One Size Does Not Fit All

One Size Does Not Fit All

Traditional and Innovative Models of Student Affairs Practice

KATHLEEN MANNING
JILLIAN KINZIE
JOHN SCHUH

Routledge
Taylor & Francis Group
New York   London

Published in 2006 by
Routledge
Taylor & Francis Group
270 Madison Avenue
New York, NY 10016

Published in Great Britain by
Routledge
Taylor & Francis Group
2 Park Square
Milton Park, Abingdon
Oxon OX14 4RN

© 2006 by Taylor & Francis Group, LLC
Routledge is an imprint of Taylor & Francis Group

10 9 8 7 6 5 4 3

International Standard Book Number-10: 0-415-95257-3 (Hardcover) 0-415-95258-1 (Softcover)
International Standard Book Number-13: 978-0-415-95257-6 (Hardcover) 978-0-415-95258-3 (Softcover)
Library of Congress Card Number 2005023068

Library of Congress Cataloging-in-Publication Data

Manning, Kathleen, 1954-
    One size does not fit all : traditional and innovative models of student affairs practice / Kathleen Manning, Jillian Kinzie, and John Schuh.
        p. cm.
    Includes bibliographical references and index.
    ISBN 0-415-95257-3 (hb : alk. paper) -- ISBN 0-415-95258-1 (pb : alk. paper)
    1. Student affairs services--United States. I. Kinzie, Jillian (Jillian L.) II. Schuh, John H. III. Title.

LB2342.92.M36 2006
378.1'94'0973--dc22   2005023068

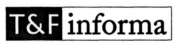

Taylor & Francis Group
is the Academic Division of T&F Informa plc.

Visit the Taylor & Francis Web site at
http://www.taylorandfrancis.com

and the Routledge Web site at
http://www.routledge-ny.com

CONTENTS

PREFACE   vii

PART I   INTRODUCTION   1

CHAPTER 1   ORGANIZING STUDENT AFFAIRS: A GLANCE IN THE REARVIEW
            MIRROR AND A LOOK AHEAD   3

CHAPTER 2   STUDENT ENGAGEMENT AND SUCCESS: RELATIONSHIPS TO
            STUDENT AFFAIRS MODELS AND PRACTICE   21

PART II   TRADITIONAL MODELS OF STUDENT AFFAIRS
            DEPARTMENTS AND DIVISIONS   35

CHAPTER 3   OUT-OF-CLASSROOM-CENTERED ESTABLISHED MODELS   37

CHAPTER 4   ADMINISTRATIVE-CENTERED ESTABLISHED MODELS   57

CHAPTER 5   LEARNING-CENTERED MODELS   77

PART III   INNOVATIVE PROPOSED MODELS BASED ON
            DEEP RESEARCH   95

CHAPTER 6 STUDENT-CENTERED INNOVATIVE MODELS   97

CHAPTER 7 ACADEMIC AND COLLABORATION INNOVATIVE MODELS   121

PART IV   WEAVING THE BASKET: PUTTING IT ALL TOGETHER   143

CHAPTER 8 COLLABORATION, STUDENT ENGAGEMENT, AND THE
            FUTURE OF STUDENT AFFAIRS PRACTICE   145

APPENDIX: RESEARCH METHOD   161

REFERENCES   167

ABOUT THE AUTHORS   179

INDEX   181

Preface

In 1997, I was invited to Colgate University, a selective liberal arts institution in upstate New York. Over lunch, a staff member gave me feedback about the way we (understood by me as faculty in graduate preparation programs) prepared new professionals for the field. I am paraphrasing, but she said,

> You educate students as if student affairs were the same at all institutions. Because you teach at a research institution, your graduates come to us understanding student affairs in that setting. I wish you would include more about what it is like to do student affairs at a competitive, liberal arts institution like ours.

Needless to say, her words haunted me for years.

Fast forward to 2003, when John Schuh, Jillian Kinzie, and I were research team members visiting a small, highly competitive liberal arts institution for the Documenting Effective Educational Practices (DEEP) project. During this visit, we were struck by the fact that student affairs at this institution was profoundly different from others we knew. Programming was deemphasized; "student affairs" referred to ways in which staff members' work was closely integrated with the academic mission; students talked about the ways their lives were academically centered; and faculty offices, not the residence halls, were the center of activity on campus. This visit started a two-year conversation about perspectives on student affairs practice that were missing from the student affairs literature. After several more site visits and conversations, the models represented in this book emerged nearly effortlessly from our thinking and the data. The time was ripe to discuss the different kinds, as opposed to kind, of student affairs practices.

The purpose of this book is to delineate models for student affairs practice. Beyond the introductory information, this book is divided into two parts: traditional models and innovative models. The first of these sections discusses student affairs models with which we are all likely familiar. These models are discussed in the standard student affairs literature, although they are rarely discussed as one of the models from which to choose. Instead, they are discussed as the "way" student affairs is carried out. The next section outlines innovative models of student affairs, which may look *very* familiar to some student affairs educators. Many of these models have been in existence at institutions but have rarely been clearly delineated in the field. Instead, they have been treated as "exceptions" if they have been discussed at all.

The student affairs field has grown tremendously over the past 20 years. The literature is more complete, our roles more clearly defined, and our practice is more finely honed. This book represents that growth. But, student affairs remains a grassroots field in which some believe there is little need for theory or conceptual models to organize practice. Similar to other areas of education, people both within and outside the field believe that common sense, rather than theoretical expertise, can.guide high-quality student affairs practice. From this perspective, models for student affairs practice are often a comfortable blend of the aforementioned common sense and administrative or managerial structural legacies. These legacies, vestiges from the past, are, according to some who practice in the field, all that is necessary to effectively lead in student affairs. Fortunately, research and administrative development in the student affairs field continue to render this commonsense approach obsolete. In fact, this book, which delineates a wide range of student affairs approaches, attests to the developing sophistication of student affairs practice. One can no longer assume that one style of student affairs practice will be congruent with the mission and ways of operating for a particular institution. Highly selective liberal arts colleges require a different approach to programming, environmental management, and policy development than a large, research institution. A women's college will undoubtedly require a different developmental approach to practice than the one used in a coeducational, comprehensive public institution. For the purposes of this book, we present the models as clearly delineated, distinct models of student practice. But these models in their "pure" form rarely exist.

Regardless of whether the model is a "pure" or "hybrid" form, no longer does one size of student affairs practice fit all. Instead, institutional type, mission, and a wide variety of circumstances (including the personality and administrative style of the senior student affairs officer) all strongly influence the model employed within a student affairs division.

We hope you find yourself and your school among the models we discuss in this book. The field is probably long overdue for a more deliberate and particular treatment of student affairs on different campuses.

Kathleen Manning
Burlington, Vermont

PART I

INTRODUCTION

CHAPTER 1

ORGANIZING STUDENT AFFAIRS: A GLANCE IN THE REARVIEW MIRROR AND A LOOK AHEAD

How student affairs should be organized and where student affairs is best positioned on an institution's organizational chart are topics that have been discussed over many decades without yielding a definitive answer. Several reasons may contribute to this situation. Student affairs, as a professional endeavor, certainly is younger than the academic and business aspects of higher education in the United States, which began with the advent of higher education in the 13 colonies. To the extent that classes had to be taught, ledgers needed to be balanced, and the physical plant kept up to at least tolerable standards made these areas of endeavor (academic and business affairs) necessary. One could argue that student affairs work actually began the first time a faculty member talked with a homesick student about the transition to college, or maybe that student affairs began because presidents needed help regulating student behavior (Rhatigan, 2000). Regardless of when or why student affairs work began, Fenske (1989) provides an insightful analysis of why student affairs has struggled with its professional identity, and why its future has been in doubt from time to time. He pointed out that the primary clientele of student services, college students, are the "most transient" (p. 29) of all of an institution's constituencies. He observed that it only took five years from the height of student unrest in the late 1960s for students to be characterized as an uninvolved generation that "adhered to political conservatism" (p. 29). Fenske argued,

> In contrast, faculty continued, largely unaffected, to teach and research in their disciplines and the institutional financial specialists likewise continued their budgeting and comptroller functions largely unaffected through the entire metamorphosis of students' attitudinal changes from materialism to involvement to indifference. (pp. 29–30)

And, there is some debate as to what constitutes student affairs. Whereas few would dispute that faculty deliver courses, evaluate student projects, and are engaged in research and other scholarly activities, or that the physical plant staff maintains institutional facilities, what constitutes student affairs work is somewhat more debatable in that functions that are part of the student affairs division on some campuses may be positioned organizationally elsewhere on others.

This chapter provides a foundation for later discussions in this book about the organization of student affairs work, and how the various approaches to student affairs we found in our study of 20 high-performing colleges and universities were developed (Kuh, Kinzie, Schuh, Whitt, & Associates, 2005). This chapter is divided into two parts. The first part provides a brief historical look at the development of student affairs with an emphasis on its organization and structure.

The second part examines selected issues that have an influence on the organization and functions of contemporary student affairs divisions of institutions of higher education.

Historical Highlights

The historical highlights provided in this section offer a quick overview of how student affairs has developed as an integral element in institutions of higher education, along with academic, business, and external affairs. From a tentative beginning, where student affairs officers were not even certain as to what their position's responsibilities would be (Rhatigan, 2000), student affairs practice has evolved into complex, sophisticated work, often involving large staffs, substantial budgets, and thousands of square feet of facilities to manage. Part of the challenge student affairs has faced over the years is to determine its niche, given that practitioners in this field are educators, managers, public relations specialists, and more. The historical highlights reflect this changing role of student affairs on many campuses to where it is today—a full partner in the education of students.

Several foundational documents laid the groundwork for the functions of student affairs practice, including *The Student Personnel Point of View, 1937* (American Council on Education [ACE], 1937) and *The Student Personnel Point of View, 1949* (ACE, 1949). "Both documents helped create an understanding of the role of student affairs in higher education" (National Association of Student Personnel Administration [NASPA], 1989, p. 5). Although a historical foundation was established nearly 70 years ago for the kinds of services, programs, activities, and experiences common on college campuses, agreement did not emerge on how these functions should be organized, to whom staff should report, and how oversight for these functions could best be provided. For example, student housing is a function that can be located in student affairs, business affairs, both, or neither (Upcraft, 1993). Other units, including enrollment management, campus recreation, intercollegiate athletics, and international programs, to name just a few, commonly found in student affairs divisions are just as often located in other administrative divisions.

The Foundation of Student Affairs

The Student Personnel Point of View, 1937 (ACE, 1937) and *The Student Personnel Point of View, 1949* (ACE, 1949) are the two most important foundational documents of the profession. These documents provided a framework for the profession, identified appropriate functions that were part of student affairs work, and established a philosophy upon which student affairs practice was developed. Prior to their adoption, individuals had served in such roles as deans of men and deans of women, and many of the functions of these individuals were quite similar to those of student affairs practitioners today (Rhatigan & Schuh, 1993), but apparently without regard to a recommended organizational structure.

The Student Personnel Point of View, 1937. The Student Personnel Point of View, 1937 (ACE, 1937), a document that shaped the core values of the profession (Nuss, 2003), identified a number of activities and functions that were part of student affairs work, but did not prescribe a specific organizational structure. The document observed, "that effective personnel work may be formally organized or may exist without direction or organization, and that frequently the informal type evidences a personnel point of view in an institution" (NASPA, 1989, p. 54). The document recommended that the functions be coordinated. In other words, "all personnel workers within an institution should cooperate with one another in order to avoid duplication of effort and in order to develop student personnel work evenly" (p. 54). But no organizational structures or organizational approaches (e.g., a freestanding unit, part of academic affairs or some other organizational structure) were recommended. The document did urge coordination between instruction and personnel work and coordination between business administration (e.g., student loans, dormitories, dining halls, and other functions related to fees and services) and personnel services. The perspective reflected in the document, particularly as "student personnel" (the document's term) related to instruction, is interesting in that the document urges a philosophy that educational institutions "consider the student as a whole" (p. 49) but that student learning be ceded to those responsible for instruction. The philosophy asserts that "an effective educational program includes in one form or another the following services adapted to the specific aims and objectives of each college and university" (p. 51). A long list of services followed this introduction, including orientation, housing, food service, extracurricular activities, supervision of social life, and so on. The authors also pointed out that new ways of organizing student personnel services were being developed, but none of these were identified specifically.

Although the authors were concerned about the education of "the student as a whole" (NASPA, 1989, p. 49), they also pointed out that "personnel offices have been appointed throughout the colleges and universities of this country to undertake a number of educational responsibilities which were once entirely assumed by teaching members of faculty" (p. 51). In effect, though, while they were concerned with the education of the "whole student," they emphasized the out-of-class experiences of students as their domain, and left student affairs practice as it related to instruction as merely a coordination function.

The Student Personnel Point of View, 1949. A dozen years after the publication of *The Student Personnel Point of View, 1937,* an updated version was published. In this document the authors identified several "generalizations" (their term) about student personnel work:

1. Campus resources were interrelated.
2. Specialized functions should be organized.
3. Equal attention should be given to process as well as administrative functions.
4. Student affairs staff should participate in institutional administration, as should students.
5. Men and women should be available in all personnel departments.
6. Programs should be evaluated.
7. Effectiveness is determined, in part, by institutional setting (pp. 39–46).

As student affairs practice (still termed "student personnel work") evolved, recommendations concerning the organization and administration of the functions under the student affairs umbrella changed to the extent that the authors recommended that "a single administrative head" (NASPA, 1989, p. 40) be appointed to lead the overall student personnel program.

Expansion and Growth

The 1950s was a decade of growth and development in student affairs. Mueller (1961) provided guidance about the administrative organization of the "personnel division," as she termed it. She indicated that a basic core of functions should be part of this division: social functions and activities, student government and disciplinary action, and student personnel records (p. 139). She added that "personnel workers will always participate in—but not have full responsibility for" (p. 139) a number of other functions, including orientation, counseling, housing, student health, placement, and admissions, to name just a few. Her advice on how these functions should be organized was very basic:

> Let us say, therefore, that on any campus a stable and well-publicized structure for personnel functions is imperative. Some centralization is necessary, and some decentralization is equally important in order to distribute the responsibilities and to reach the largest number of students directly. (1961, p. 143)

She also pointed out that faculty and students should be involved in the delivery of services and make important contributions to student affairs. Mueller emphasized that a "personnel division" was necessary on campus. She asserted:

> The main reason is that an individual, especially a professional, needs the support which a work structure gives to his [*sic*] ego-integration processes. The organization, whatever it is, identifies him to himself as well as to his colleagues, his family, his friends. It lends status, and by means of it, his superiors know where and what he is and how to give orders to him. (1961, p. 134)

The 1960s: A Tumultuous Decade

As student affairs work grew in complexity, the issue of whether or not a student affairs division should exist was resolved. Divisions of student affairs were created, perhaps in part because the issues of the day were complex and exhausting. Among them were students' feeling disaffected by the increasing size and complexity of their institutions (Thelin, 2004), civil rights (Rhatigan, 2000), issues of free speech (Caple, 1998), the Vietnam War (Thelin, 2003), and a series of court cases that challenged that position that institutions stood *in loco parentis* in their relationships with students (Caple, 1998). Sandeen (2001) pointed out that many faculty "welcomed release from what they considered bothersome advising duties or some vague responsibility for student behavior" (p. 184). Regardless, Chandler (1973/1986), while identifying some of the challenges of student affairs administration, asserted that the units comprising a student affairs division should be headed by a vice president and that student affairs should be "one of the major components of the university organization" (p. 338).

Campuses continued to grow in enrollment in the 1960s and civil unrest and controversy marked the last part of the decade. "Campus dissent became violent in a number of instances and occasionally was met by repressive responses that worsened matters" (Rhatigan, 2000, p. 19). Student affairs staff members, in the middle of this difficult period of time, were charged with keeping order on campus while at the same time preserving free speech. As contentious and violent as the decade was, "Student unrest persisted into the early 1970s but had waned by about 1973" (Thelin, 2004, p. 326).

One organizational issue that was addressed and resolved was whether student affairs should be organized using a dean of men/dean of women model. Crane (1963/1983) asserted, "The division between male and female offices is purposeful and practical" (p. 115). He urged that services for men and women ought to be kept separate. His advice did not prevail, and the offices were merged into a dean of students model, an administrative restructuring that had been urged by W.H. Cowley in 1934 (Schwartz, 2002). Deans of men, according to Schwartz, fell victim to the desire for increased efficiency as institutions of higher education grew in size and complexity, and to the increasing emphasis on the professional education of student affairs practitioners. The dean of women position was eliminated for other reasons. Schwartz

(1997) asserted that "the position of dean of women was an inevitable victim of the pervasive hostility that greeted women in general on campus, while the position of dean of men assumed new administrative importance" (p. 432). Although the position of dean of women disappeared, those who served in this role should not be forgotten, for, as Rhatigan concluded,

> We have forgotten their essential courage in the face of formidable circumstances, their dedication in attempting to open new fields of study to women; their persistence even in failure; the stereotype they rose above; the ethical standards evidenced in their work and writing; and the example they set for all who followed. (2000, pp. 10–11)

1970 to 1990: Adjustment and Accountability

Thelin (2003, p. 16) characterized the two decades from 1970 to 1990 as an era of "adjustment and accountability." A number of functions were added to the student affairs portfolio either wholly or in part. Federal legislation such as Section 504 of the Rehabilitation Act of 1973 was designed to make the campus accessible for students with disabilities who, in many cases, had not been welcome on college campuses. Title IX of the Educational Amendments of 1972 was passed to ensure that opportunities for women were equal to those of men. Who was to lead the campus response to these mandates? In some cases it was student affairs, and, consequently, the portfolio of student affairs administrators grew. But with this growth came questions of accountability. As institutions' budgets were severely tested, first by runaway inflation in the late 1970s and then by recession in the early 1980s, the question of accountability grew. How could institutions demonstrate that they were using their resources wisely? "Two-thirds of the states mandated, by legislation, that public colleges and universities adopt plans for assessing student learning" (Burke, 2004, p. 7). Questions related to accountability also were asked of student affairs units, which often tried to ignore the questions or change the subject. This may have triggered questions about where student affairs units belong in the institution's organizational structure and, perhaps more importantly, what philosophy guides student affairs practice.

Focus on Student Learning

As the 1990s unfolded, a number of important volumes were released that helped refocus student affairs. These included the works of Boyer (1987, 1990); Kuh, Schuh, Whitt, and Associates (1991); and Pascarella and Terenzini (1991). These publications advocated a renewed emphasis on the undergraduate student experience and provided empirical evidence that the out-of-class experience of students contributed substantially to their learning and growth. One could argue that these volumes set the stage for additional reports that challenged colleges and universities to reemphasize student learning. Included in this set were *The Student Learning Imperative* (American College Personnel Association [ACPA], 1996) and *Powerful Partnerships* (American Association for Higher Educatlion [AAHE], American College Personnel Association [ACPA], & National Association of Student Personnel Administrators [NASPA], 1998). The former advocated a renewed emphasis on student learning as a focus of student affairs practice. The latter suggested ways that various units of higher education could work together to enrich the student experience. Although this call for collaboration was well received by many institutions (see Schuh & Whitt, 1999), the fact is that a collaborative approach had been advocated by Shaffer in 1961 (1961/1986). Of course, if both of these documents were to have their most potent effect on the undergraduate experience, the question naturally would arise, where does student affairs belong in the organizational structure of a college or university? If learning is the emphasis, would it make sense to place student affairs within the portfolio of academic affairs, since student learning had always been the territory of faculty and academic administrators? Or would it make more sense to continue the development of separate units of student affairs (e.g., a vice president reporting to the president), which had been the case since the 1950s and 1960s when the complexity of student affairs had emerged and developed? Although the organizational locus of student affairs continued to depend on local (meaning campus-based) factors and issues, further advice related to organizational practice, particularly as it could advance student learning, was provided in the document *Principles of Good Practice* (ACPA/NASPA, 1997/1999). The authors reported that the principles contained in this document were designed to "guide the daily practice of student affairs work" (ACPA/NASPA, 2004, p. 1).

Factors Affecting the Organization of Student Affairs

A number of current issues have had an effect on the organization of the current student affairs division. Sandeen identified a set of factors that influence how a student affairs division is organized, but added, "There is no single organizational model that fits every institution" (2001, p. 187). Included in his factors are institutional mission and culture, professional background of the student affairs staff, student characteristics, presidents and senior academic officers, academic organization, financial resources, technology, and legislation and court decisions. He concluded,

> There is no standard structure that can fit all institutions equally well, and an organizational model that worked effectively 10 years ago may need significant realignment to be effective today. Student affairs administrators should view the organizational structure as a vehicle for carrying out their educational, leadership, management and service goals. (p. 208)

Thus, Sandeen called for periodic review of organizational relationships and functions, so that student affairs remains contemporary in its organization and functions.

Given that a wide variety of factors influence what student affairs units do and how they are organized, are there common models for student affairs organization and practice? Dungy (2003) observed, "Traditionally, student affairs has been a stand-alone division with the senior student affairs administrator reporting to the president, whether the organizational structure was centralized or decentralized" (p. 340). But she also pointed out that some institutions have combined academic and student affairs into one unit, headed by the provost or vice president for academic affairs, and she acknowledged some institutions where this organizational arrangement was in place but had reverted to a freestanding student affairs division with the senior student affairs officer reporting directly to the president.

Oversight for student affairs is another organizational issue ripe for debate. Should the senior student affairs officer (often titled vice president for student affairs [VPSA] for the purpose of this discussion) report directly to the senior institutional officer (president) or the senior academic officer (provost)? Ambler provides various perspectives on this subject, but in the end concluded (Ambler, 2000),

> The relationship of the student affairs organization to the institutional organization as a whole is very important, but it is not as critical to the success of student affairs as the relationships, coalitions, and cooperative programs that can be developed. (pp. 133–134)

Conceptualization of Student Affairs

At least three different approaches to student affairs work that also affect the organization of student affairs have emerged over the years. These include student services, student development, and student learning. In some respects, these approaches to conceptualizing student affairs are quite similar to an analysis of student affairs philosophical documents conducted by Evans and Reason (2001), who concluded that student learning, development of students, and service to students are clear themes of the 13 foundational student affairs documents they analyzed.

Student Services. Although not taking the format of a fast food operation feared by Crane (1963/1983), this concept of student affairs practice, in effect, holds that student affairs provides a collection of services to students that are part of their experience. But these experiences largely stand independent of one another, without much thought given to the total student experience. Some might think of it as a medical model, in that if students are interested in exercise, they can use the facilities of the recreation building. If they catch a cold, they go to the health service for treatment. If they want to establish an organization, they can go to student activities for a list of procedures they need to follow in filing a constitution and receive financial support. Under this conceptualization of student affairs, the units in student affairs are loosely coordinated, and one could make the case that they could be scattered around the administrative landscape without much effect on their performance.

Student Development. In this way of conceptualizing student affairs, the units of student affairs work together to provide a coherent, cohesive out-of-class learning experience for students. So, a student who is interested in diet might consult with the student health service wellness coordinator but also work with an exercise consultant in the recreation program and touch base with the food service nutritionist on diet issues. The staff of these units would work together to provide a coordinated set of experiences to help students achieve their goals. This approach might be guided by a psychosocial theory of student growth, with the recognition that the learning that occurs in the classroom is the domain of faculty. This conceptualization of student affairs is likely to be organized as a freestanding division of the institution.

Student Learning. This concept of student affairs conceptualizes the student experience as an integrated, coordinated series of experiences that begins when a prospective student contacts the institution for information about applying for admission. Campus visits for prospective students are coordinated with faculty. Residential programs involve faculty. Courses for students new to the institution (first-year students or transfers) are co-taught by student affairs staff and faculty. This concept of student affairs work lends itself to partnerships being formed regularly to advance the student experience. It also calls into question if the units that are typically found in a student affairs division ought to be part of the senior academic officer's portfolio or freestanding. A case can be made for either, but the guiding question that is used to frame the work of these units is, how will what we do contribute to what students learn? (See chapters 6 and 8.)

Institutional Mission

Lyons (1993) offered a particularly insightful commentary on what influences student affairs work by his assertion that "the most important factor that determines the shape and substance of student affairs is the mission of the institution" (p. 14). He added that

> how the work of student affairs is structured, how its responsibilities are defined, how it is valued, and how it relates to the work and culture of an institution can vary greatly from one university to another and even within an institution. (p. 14)

Lyons's perspective provides a foundation for thinking about how student affairs ought to be organized and how the work of student affairs staff can contribute to advancing the institution with which they are affiliated.

Building on the work of Lyons, Barr (2000) identified factors that influence an institution's mission, and, hence, that of student affairs. These included such factors as an institution's affiliation; its characteristics, history, focus, and governance; whether it is part of a system; the geographic location; and whether it is linked to other institutions through such activities as shared library facilities or dual enrollment policies. In the end she asserted, "Full understanding of the institutional mission statement is essential to development of sound and effective student affairs programs and services" (p. 35). Sandeen (2001) agreed with that premise in his conclusion that "the student affairs organizational structure always should reflect the dominant emphasis of the institution" (p. 204).

Doyle (2004) surveyed 216 chief student affairs officers chosen at random from four-year colleges and universities with an enrollment of 500 to 3,000 students in 2001. His questionnaire was based on the *Principles of Good Practice* published by NASPA and ACPA in 1997. Among his recommendations was the following: "If student affairs wants not only to survive, but also to prosper, it must demonstrate to the rest of the institution that it holds itself accountable for achieving not only the division's mission, but also the institution's mission" (p. 391). Doyle concluded that student affairs must do a better job of using resources to effectively achieve institutional missions and goals.

Hirt, Amelink, and Schneiter (2004) studied the nature of student affairs work in liberal arts colleges (LACs). They found that student affairs practice differed at LACs compared with that at other types of institutions. They concluded, "Overall, student affairs work at LACs is collaborative, team-oriented, positively challenging and often requires professionals to take on additional responsibilities" (p. 102). Hirt et al. recommended that graduate preparation programs use these findings "to illustrate how institutional environments vary and how those differences affect what student affairs professionals do" (pp. 106–107).

In one situation of financial exigency, a student affairs division focused on how it contributed to the institution's mission. Scott and Bischoff (2000) reported how budget cuts were managed at Ramapo College of New Jersey. They concluded, "The pivotal role played by Student Affairs in advancing the primary purposes of the institution led the college's leadership team to reject the option of disproportionately downsizing the division of Student Affairs, although that had been the response to financial pressures involved by substantial numbers of other institutions nationwide" (p. 124, citing Cage, 1992). They added, "The student affairs operation of the future must be a nimble and flexible organization, skilled in meeting rapidly changing and evolving student needs" (p. 131).

Ballou (1997) reported another example of reorganization. In this case the reorganization of student affairs was undertaken to affect savings and serve students more effectively. In this reorganization, departments were eliminated, student affairs was placed under the supervision of the senior academic officer, and "an equally strong emphasis is placed on the role of Student Affairs in directly supporting student learning. Students' success in the classroom is of primary importance" (1997, p. 25).

Developing an Organization to Support Student Learning

One of the current strategies for organizing student affairs considers the extent to which the student affairs division supports and enhances student learning. Blimling, Whitt, and Associates (1999) asserted the following: "We believe that student affairs organizations must reaffirm their commitment to being student centered and continue to press for institutions to redefine their mission in terms of students and what student learn" (p. 187). Building on the principles of good practice, Doyle examined how student affairs "might integrate the practice associated with student learning" (2004, p. 378). He found that "student affairs divisions were most successful at incorporating principles of learning based on direct interaction with students, including (1) engaging students in active learning, (2) helping students develop coherent values and (3) building supportive and inclusive communities" (p. 375). But, he cautioned "student affairs divisions may be excellent at building good relationships with students that improve learning but less adept at creating a management structure that enhances learning" (p. 388).

Kezar (2003a) studied collaboration between academic and student affairs, focusing on structural and cultural strategies by surveying 260 randomly selected senior student affairs officers. On the basis of responses from 128 participants, she concluded, "Both structural and cultural strategies appear important for creating change on campus and support a blended approach to change. . . . Cultural strategies are most often successfully used" (p. 16). In another report, Kezar (2003b) observed that institutions with enrollments of more than 10,000 need to rely less on leadership and more on planning and restructuring in creating partnerships between academic and student affairs divisions, which is another organizational approach designed to support student learning.

Forming Partnerships. Student affairs has responded to the call for increasing the emphasis on student learning by embracing several documents, including *The Student Learning Imperative* (Schroeder, 2003). One of the ways Schroeder suggested to achieve an effective, institution-wide approach to student learning is the development of partnerships between academic and student affairs. He concluded, "If colleges and universities are to address successfully the multitude of internal and external challenges they currently face, personnel in academic and student affairs must choose, as Rosa Parks chose, to live divided no more" (1999b, p. 16). Schroeder (2003) identified a number of barriers to collaboration between academic and student affairs: (a) fundamental cultural differences, (b) lack of mutual understanding and respect, (c) fragmented organizational structures, (d) tyranny of custom, and (e) lack of knowledge and shared vision of undergraduate education. He observed that breaking down these barriers will take "time, energy and commitment" (2003, p. 625). Beyond these features, he also identified a series of strategies that "can be very useful in the creation of effective partnerships" (p. 626):

1. Partnerships are usually most successful when they are developed from a common reference point or common purpose.
2. It is necessary to identify potential partners who have a common commitment to address the issues, an understanding of relevant

campus operation, and the authority to institute and support changes.

3. They usually involve cross-functional teams, joint planning, and implementation and assessment of mutually agreed-upon outcomes.

4. They often require new perspectives, such as thinking and acting systematically by linking, aligning, and integrating a variety of resources.

5. They also require participants to step out of their comfort zone, challenge prevailing assumptions and take reasonable risks.

6. They require senior administrators to be strong champions and advocates for innovation and change.

7. Building partnerships is hard work that necessitates perseverance and tenacity (pp. 626–628).

So, one important feature in thinking about the student affairs organization of the future is the extent to which the organizational structure and culture will provide the nimbleness and flexibility to create partnerships as appropriate to advance student learning. What might examples of these partnerships be? Obvious examples are partnerships that provide learning components to such traditional student affairs functions as residential life, student activities, orientation, and student health services. Who exactly comes together to form these partnerships will depend on the exigencies of the individual institution, but the partnerships certainly have the potential to add richness to the student learning experience more so than if the various units went about their work independently.

In spite of the challenges to forming partnerships, success stories are available to serve as models in forming partnerships that serve students well and ultimately enhance learning. Ballard and Long (2004) provide advice on how to focus an entire institution on student learning, of which collaboration between academic and student affairs is an essential ingredient. In developing goals for their university, the first goal centered on students and required collaboration between academic and student affairs. A telling observation came from the provost: "When I evaluated our academic programs related to student success, it became clear to me that Academic Affairs must do more and we could not be successful without a strong partnership with Student Affairs" (p. 17).

A programmatic example of the development of a partnership is the formation of a joint initiative between an academic department (psychology) and a women's center to provide sexual assault education, prevention, and victim services (Yeater, Miltenberger, Laden, Ellis, & O'Donohue, 2001). The authors concluded, "this collaboration has produced a number of new and exciting benefits on the UNR campus, and continues to do so" (p. 448).

Engstrom and Tinto identified learning communities and service learning as initiatives that "embrace the principles of collaborative learning and have the potential to transform our institutions into true learning-centered organizations" (2000, p. 436). They also identified other activities, including "freshmen experience programs, retention efforts, career development initiatives leadership development or multiculturalism" as "promising collaborative partnerships" (p. 436). They concluded that such factors as "mutual respect, equality, trust, and shared learning" (p. 448) are important ingredients in the development of partnerships between student affairs and faculty.

Merging with Academic Affairs. An alternative to forming partnerships with academic affairs is for student affairs to be organizationally merged or combined with academic affairs. Price (1999) provides observations about what this experience meant for the student affairs division with which he was associated. He raised a number of questions about a possible merger that ought to be considered. Among them are the following:

1. Is the merger initiated by the possibility of budget savings or an enhanced, integrated learning environment?
2. Is the provost committed to interaction among student affairs staff and deans and academic staff?
3. Will the provost be an advocate for out-of-class learning to the president and other institutional leaders?
4. Are student affairs staff and academic administrators willing to abandon their traditional roles and take risks that might cause discomfort?

5. Are key quality-of-life functions (housing, food service, student union) under the supervision of business affairs?

6. Does the senior business officer value student affairs and out-of-class learning?

7. Does the president have experience with or value student affairs and out-of-class learning (p. 81)?

Conclusion

This chapter provides a brief perspective on the organizational development of student affairs over the years. As the functions of student affairs were developed and refined, no universal organizational model has emerged. Rather, student affairs evolved from a dean of men/dean of women model to a dean of students model, but beyond that how the division of student affairs is organized and to whom it reports have been influenced largely by the history, culture, and needs of specific institutions. Contrasted with academic affairs and business affairs, student affairs has struggled to find its place within the organizational structure of colleges and universities.

Various perspectives on how student affairs should be organized, to whom student affairs should report, and precisely what functions should be included in the student affairs portfolio, are likely to be the focus of spirited debate in the future. What is clear is that there is no one best way to do "student affairs," but rather, the effectiveness of the activities of student affairs units will be determined by a variety of factors, including some of those described in this chapter.

CHAPTER 2

STUDENT ENGAGEMENT AND SUCCESS: RELATIONSHIPS TO STUDENT AFFAIRS MODELS AND PRACTICE

Concern about student success in college has never been greater. Legislative bodies, accreditation commissions, and the broader public have scrutinized institutional graduation rates, questioned persistent graduation rate gaps among different student populations, unequivocally called for improvements in the undergraduate experience, and insisted on greater accountability for student learning outcomes. The demand for evidence of student learning and institutional effectiveness has steadily increased since the mid-1980s, when several influential reports appeared, beginning with *A Nation at Risk* (National Commission on Excellence in Education, 1983) and its postsecondary counterpart, *Involvement in Learning* (Study Group on the Conditions of Excellence in American Higher Education, 1984).

According to Smith (2004), too many people of all incomes and races fail to thrive in our institutions because colleges and universities lack the capacity to educate. Moreover, a recent report by the Education Trust exposed serious shortfalls in college graduation rates: nearly 20% of four-year institutions in the United States graduate less than one third of their first-time, full-time, degree-seeking first-year students within six years (Carey, 2004). Coincident with these pressures, higher education has become more widely available to students, with an increasing proportion of high school graduates and working adults attending college (Kirp, 2003). As a result, many colleges and universities are demonstrating how they achieve high-quality undergraduate education as well as enhance and document student success to a wide range of constituents.

The Link Among Engagement, Learning, and Student Success

Several widely disseminated publications lay out the key concepts associated with student success and effective institutional performance, including "The Seven Principles for Good Practices in Undergraduate Education" (Chickering & Gamson, 1987) and Education Commission of the States's (1995) *Making Quality Count in Undergraduate Education*, which fleshes out related factors and conditions in more detail. These publications plainly indicate that colleges and universities have a responsibility to do more to foster student learning. Kuh et al., (2005) assert that "educationally effective colleges and universities—those that add value—channel students' energies toward appropriate activities and engage them at a high level in these activities" (p. 9). The consistent message across these volumes is that enhancing student success should be the main priority at all institutions of higher education. Broadly defined, student success in college encompasses academic achievement; engagement in educationally purposeful activities; satisfaction; acquisition of desired knowledge, skills, and competencies; persistence; educational attainment; and postcollege performance.

Student affairs organizations have issued similar calls for increased focus on student learning as primary undergraduate goals. The push for reform outlined in the ACPA's (1996) *Student Learning Imperative* focused on total student learning as an institution's principal academic mission. More recent reports, such as "The Residential Nexus" (Association of College and University Housing Officers-International Residential College Task Force, 1996) recommended that student learning outcome goals influence administrative functions and programmatic models in campus housing. *Powerful Partnerships: A Shared Responsibility for Learning* (AAHE et al., 1998) outlined principles for possible collaborations for student learning. *Learning Reconsidered* (ACPA & NASPA, 2004) promoted the integration of all higher education resources to educate and prepare the whole student.

These publications sound a common call for specific actions and collaborations to raise the quality of student learning in college. Together, they point to the following institutional conditions important to student success: (a) a clear, focused institutional mission, (b) high standards for student performance, (c) support for students to explore human differences and emerging dimensions of self, (d) emphasis on the first college year, (e) respect for diverse talents, (f) integration of prior learning and experience, (g) ongoing application of learned skills, (h) learning-centered pedagogy, (i) active learning, (j) integrative culminating experiences, (k) assessment and feedback, (l) collaboration between student and academic affairs and among students, (m) quality time on task, and (n) out-of-class contact with faculty. Many of these practices have taken root to varying degrees in colleges and universities across the country. For example, most institutions concentrate resources on first-year students. Other institutions established learning communities, particularly at urban and commuter campuses, as an effective way to connect students to their peers and faculty. Service learning and related forms of community involvement have gained prominence in the undergraduate experience. These types of university programs and practices increase student engagement (defined as the time and energy students devote to educationally purposeful activities) as well as lead to greater institutional effectiveness and, ultimately, student success.

Student engagement is a key component to student success. What students do during college, the extent to which they are engaged in activities that research indicates contributes to learning and personal development, matters to student persistence and success (Kuh, 2001a, 2003; National Survey of Student Engagement [NESSE], 2002, 2003a). Therefore, educationally effective institutions, those that align practice and policy around student engagement, are more likely to realize higher levels of student success (Kuh et al., 2005). In addition, the effect is greater when these practices are linked and integrated.

Although we have some sense of what is emblematic of educationally engaging and effective practice, it is helpful to extend this view to images of what student affairs looks like from a student engagement and success perspective. What are the features of a student success–oriented model for student affairs? Is there one best model? In this chapter an exploration of research-based models for student affairs practice is introduced in three parts. First, the student success framework that anchors the work and defines the important components of student engagement is outlined. Second, the links between student engagement and success and student affairs models are made explicit. Third, the research that provided data and ample inspiration to think deeply about models for student affairs practice is described. The chapter concludes with insights into student affairs practice at educationally effective institutions.

The Concept of Student Engagement

At the nexus of concern about student success and institutional effectiveness is student engagement. Research on the impact of college on students shows that the time and energy students devote to educationally purposeful activities is an important predictor of their learning and personal development (Astin, 1993; Pace, 1980; Pascarella & Terenzini, 1991, 2005). Simply put, what students *do* during college has a greater influence on what they learn and whether they graduate than *who* they are or even *where* they go to college (Kuh, 2001b, 2003;

NSSE, 2002, 2003a). Pascarella and Terenzini (2005) reaffirmed that the impact of college is primarily determined by individual student effort and involvement in the curricular and co-curricular offerings on a campus.

> Students are not passive recipients of institutional efforts to "educate" or "change" them but rather bear a major responsibility for any gains derived from their postsecondary experience. This is not to say that an individual campus's ethos, policies, and programs are unimportant; quite the contrary. But if, as it appears, individual effort or engagement is the critical determinant of the impact of college, then it is important to focus on the ways in which an institution can shape its academic, interpersonal, and extracurricular offerings to encourage student engagement. (Pascarella & Terenzini, 2005, p. 602)

According to Kuh (2001b), the concept of student engagement originates from Pace's (1982) measures of quality of effort and Astin's (1985) theory of involvement. Student engagement represents two key components. The first is the amount of time and effort students put into their studies and activities that lead to the experiences and outcomes that constitute student success. Second is how institutions of higher education allocate their human and other resources as well as how they organize learning opportunities and services to encourage students to participate in and benefit from such activities. Since colleges and universities have a direct influence over the institutional conditions and practices that foster student success, this second dimension of engagement represents a point of influence for institutions.

Student engagement is associated with many of the desired processes and outcomes of higher education. For example, high levels of student engagement are associated with a wide range of educational practices and conditions including purposeful student-faculty contact and active and collaborative learning. Student engagement occurs when institutional environments are perceived by students as supportive and affirming and where expectations for performance are clearly communicated and set at reasonably high levels (Astin, 1991; Chickering & Gamson, 1987; Chickering & Reisser, 1993; Kuh, 2003; Kuh et al., 1991; Pascarella, 2001; Pascarella & Terenzini, 1991, 2005). These and other factors and conditions are related to student satisfaction, learning and development, persistence, and educational attainment (Astin, 1984, 1985, 1993; Bruffee, 1993; Goodsell, Maher, & Tinto, 1992; Johnson, Johnson, & Smith, 1991; McKeachie, Pintrich, Lin, & Smith, 1986; Pascarella & Terenzini, 1991, 2005; Pike, 1993; Sorcinelli, 1991).

The National Survey of Student Engagement

Since 2000, the NSSE has provided an assessment of (a) the extent to which students are engaged in empirically derived high-quality educational practices, and (b) what they gain from their college experience (Kuh, 2001b). The survey broadly documents dimensions of quality in undergraduate education. Student engagement measures have been positively correlated with educational gains, grades, retention, satisfaction, and graduation rates (see Hu & Kuh, 2002; Kuh, 2003; Pascarella & Terenzini, 2005). These findings demonstrate the promise of efforts to increase student engagement. Moreover, student engagement results can assist administrators and faculty to understand and enhance student success. Survey results can point to areas of the undergraduate experience where institutions can effect change and impact the extent to which students are involved in educationally effective practice (NSSE, 2003a, 2004a). This emphasis assists faculty, staff, administrators, students, and others identify the tasks and activities associated with higher yields in areas of desired student outcomes. Beyond the practical value of the survey data, the NSSE project has helped introduce the language of effective practice, student engagement, and quality in undergraduate education into higher education institutions (Kuh, 2003).

Although most colleges claim to offer high-quality learning environments for students, few can directly demonstrate their impact on student learning (Kuh, 2001a; Miller & Ewell, 2004). Instead, many institutions point to educationally enriching opportunities they make available (e.g., honors programs, co-curricular leadership development programs, and collaboration on faculty research) as evidence for high-quality learning. However, many of the experiences are limited to small numbers of students. In effect, these experiences leave larger populations disconnected from peers and educators and excluded from enhanced learning experiences (Kuh et al., 2005). Consequently, students are less likely to get meaningfully engaged in learning and more likely to leave college prematurely. Institutions can be more intentional about encouraging more students to participate in educationally purposeful activities.

Student Success and Student Affairs

Student engagement is an important precursor to student success. Student success is broadly defined as retention, graduation, and educational attainment (Kuh et al., 2005). Thus, successful students persist, benefit in desired ways from the college experiences, are satisfied with college, and graduate. Although policy makers and legislators may define student success more precisely as the percentage of students who earn a college degree in four years, other educators and researchers define student success as the extent to which students make gains in critical thinking, effective reasoning and problem solving, application of knowledge, inclination to inquire, integration of learning, and leadership. Despite the differences in definitions of student success, all are dependent on students being engaged in educationally purposeful activities.

The inclusion of educational gains and learning outcomes as determinants of student success is characteristic of a student-centered learning paradigm (see chapters 5 and 6). According to Tagg (2003), the learning paradigm college is one in which the institutional mission is to create conditions that produce learning, not simply deliver instruction. In the learning paradigm, the focus is on the quality of *exiting* students and their learning skills and not the quality of *entering* students. In this framework, student success results in colleges and universities that focus on developing students' talents.

Student growth and development have long been goals of student affairs. As discussed in chapter 1, a central commitment of student affairs practice expressed in the statement of *Principles of Good Practice for Student Affairs* (ACPA & NASPA, 1997) is the development of the whole person. This value incorporates a belief in the appreciation of individual differences, lifelong learning, and education for citizenship, assessment, and pluralism. Moreover, *The Student Learning Imperative* (ACPA, 1996) pointed out the importance of student affairs professionals working cooperatively with academic affairs both in and out

of the classroom to foster student learning. These student affairs principles are not only congruent with contemporary trends in education,
such as the learning paradigm, but align with a comprehensive view of
student success as the promotion of student learning and development.
A student success perspective creates a context in which student affairs
enacts its educational role and influence.

The Role of Student Affairs in Persistence

Student affairs often has been assigned responsibility for persistence—
an early and essential factor in student success. In fact, for decades, many
colleges and universities have delegated student retention programs
and other student success initiatives to student affairs professionals
(Tinto, 1996). Many of these programs, including extended orienta-
tions, developmental courses, and enhanced programming in residence
halls, are created and staffed by student affairs practitioners and are not
integrated with the academic experience. This practice is problematic
if it absolves other institutional units of the responsibility for student
persistence and concern for student success. However, student affairs
professionals at most colleges and universities are well positioned to
establish the campus conditions that affirm students as well as provide
the programs and services to meet their academic and social needs
outside the classroom. For example, new student orientation and fall
welcome-week activities equip students with the skills they need to
acclimate. Peer mentoring, study groups, and tutoring programs foster
interdependent learning. Notably, persistence efforts are even more
effective when accomplished in full partnership with academic affairs
and other institutional support structures.

Although a number of the programs and other initiatives listed
above, such as residence hall programs, student activities, and orientation, have been part of the student affairs portfolio for years, other
programs have emerged in more recent times that also contribute to
student persistence and have been assigned to student affairs wholly or
in part. Many of these student experiences were found at DEEP project institutions, which will be described later in this chapter. Among
them were learning communities, service learning and volunteer experiences, study abroad, leadership development, undergraduate research

opportunities, diversity initiatives, tutorial programs, and capstone experiences. Assuming that these student experiences will be implemented at increasing numbers of colleges and universities and enriched on campuses where they already exist, one of the challenges for institutional leaders is to position them organizationally where they can have the greatest impact on the largest number of students. Lessons can be learned from DEEP institutions about how to make these organizational decisions.

The involvement of student affairs in student success and persistence is congruent with the traditional mission of student affairs. The profession's underpinnings emphasize concern about students, including the promotion of student development and learning, acquisition of leadership skills, appreciation of diversity, and attention to retention. Despite a direct role in student persistence, there have been many calls for reform in student affairs related to collaborating with academic affairs, enhancing student learning outcomes, and affirming student affairs contributions to the educational mission. These reform efforts indicate that student affairs practice can do more to promote student success, persistence, and graduation.

Student Engagement and Success: A Framework for Exploring Student Affairs Models

In the preceding sections, the relationship between student affairs, student engagement, and success was drawn. These concepts form the basis for the student affairs models for practice discussed in this book. Our interest in and examination of student affairs models originated in the context of the DEEP project (see preface). DEEP was an 18-month study to understand successful educational practices at 20 different colleges and universities—all of which had higher than predicted student engagement scores, as measured by the NSSE, and higher than predicted graduation rates (see the appendix for an explanation of the methodology). Findings from the project and details about the methodology employed can be found in *Student Success in College: Creating Conditions That Matter* (Kuh et al., 2005).

Specifically, the examination of student affairs practice from a student success framework began with the expectation that educationally effective institutions have distinct approaches to student affairs practice. In fact, one simple question launched our examination: Is there an ideal model for student affairs practice at educationally engaging institutions? The following questions furthered our examination of student affairs practice:

1. What does student affairs look like at colleges and universities with high levels of student engagement?
2. What role does student affairs play in promoting student success and, in particular, higher than predicted graduation rates?
3. What similarities in student affairs practice exist across institutions that promote student success well?
4. Is it possible that widely divergent approaches to student affairs can work equally well to foster student success?
5. How do these approaches differ from established student affairs models?

Although the DEEP research project was not designed as a study of student affairs, as we visited institutions, conducted fieldwork, and interviewed respondents, we began to take note of and scrutinize approaches to student affairs at these institutions. In fact, several members of the research team theorized independently about the distinctiveness of student affairs units at DEEP institutions. During data collection and analysis, we found ourselves reflecting on the characteristics and trends in student affairs that warranted additional investigation. Toward this end, we reconsidered the DEEP data and project findings with an eye toward developing an enriched understanding of student affairs practice in educationally effective institutions with higher than predicted student engagement and graduation rates.

The DEEP Study

Since the DEEP research served as a touchstone for the models presented in this book, a brief introduction to the project is in order. The DEEP research originated from a concern that, despite an ample body of research demonstrating the importance of student engagement and effective educational practice, many colleges and universities have little experience in intentionally creating the conditions that promote student success. In addition, few schools have effective mechanisms for linking information about student experiences to efforts to improve academic programs and student support services. However, some colleges and universities are clearly doing better than others in the creation of powerful student success–oriented learning cultures. The research approach for the DEEP project was influenced by a time-honored practice in the for-profit sector: study high-performing organizations and adapt the most effective practices. Valuable lessons can be learned from organizations that stand out for their effectiveness. This principle is useful for higher education since information about what works in undergraduate education can help all institutions improve the conditions for student success. In sum, DEEP discovered and described the policies and practices of institutions with strong records of student success and documented and shared the practices that enhance the quality of undergraduate experiences. (See the appendix for sampling procedures.) The DEEP project launched in 2002 through the support of Lumina Foundation for Education, the Center of Inquiry in the Liberal Arts at Wabash College, and the AAHE.

To have achieved higher than predicted levels of engagement and graduation represents something meaningful beyond students' entering characteristics. Specifically, students at these institutions take greater advantage of the educational opportunities than students at other institutions (Kuh et al., 2005). Although these institutions are certainly doing well by their students, it is important to note the caution issued in *Student Success in College* (Kuh et al., 2005). DEEP institutions are not the "best" or the "most educationally effective" of the more than 700 four-year colleges and universities that had participated in NSSE by 2003 (the potential sample of institutions for inclusion in DEEP). Yet their performance is noteworthy, and they offer many examples of promising practices that could be adapted at other institutions.

Student Success in College (Kuh et al., 2005) provides extensive illustrations of the specific practices and cultural features at the DEEP institutions that contribute to student success. Many of the practices employed at these institutions were innovative, homegrown ideas that clearly distinguished the institution. The University of Maine at Farmington's Student Work Initiative was created to fund more on-campus jobs so that their mostly first-generation students who had to work while attending college could do so while establishing meaningful connections to faculty, peers, and staff on campus. Resident assistants at Longwood University were trained to introduce new students to the educational mission of the institution as well as provide peer advising and academic support in the residence halls. The learning communities established at the University of Texas at El Paso facilitated peer interaction among the institution's predominately commuter students. These practices were thoughtfully designed with the institutional context and students' needs in mind.

Although many of the DEEP schools developed unique programs to facilitate student success, what is perhaps good news for all colleges and universities is that many of the successful programs found at DEEP schools exist in some form at most colleges and universities. For instance, several DEEP schools had great success with first-year seminar programs, mentoring programs, student and academic affairs collaborations, undergraduate research programs, and learning communities. *However, what sets the DEEP schools apart is the range and quality of their initiatives, the extent to which all students are touched by enriched educational experiences, and the degree to which practices are integrated and linked to one another.*

In addition to documenting specific educational programs and practices like those described above, the DEEP research team also identified six overarching conditions and properties that were shared by these institutions. The six conditions for educational effectiveness (see Table 2.1) are interdependent elements that work in complementary ways to promote student success.

The importance of several of these conditions is immediately obvious. For example, it is not surprising that DEEP schools enact an "unshakeable focus on student learning." Student learning is at the core of daily activities of everyone on campus. Student affairs professionals at Miami University work collaboratively with academic affairs administrators to ensure an array of educationally enriched opportunities in their living-learning communities. These six properties and conditions accompanied by the effective educational practices demonstrate the breadth of practices associated with student success. If adapted appropriately,

Table 2.1 Six Conditions That Matter to Student Success

1. "Living" Mission and "Lived" Educational Philosophy

2. Unshakeable Focus on Student Learning

3. Environments Adapted for Educational Enrichment

4. Clear Pathways to Student Success

5. Improvement-Oriented Ethos

6. Shared Responsibility for Educational Quality and Student Success

Source: Kuh, Kinzie, Schuh, Whitt, and Associates (2005). *Student Success in College: Creating Conditions That Matter.* San Francisco: Jossey–Bass.

these conditions enable colleges and universities to create and sustain cultures that support student success.

The elaboration of effective educational practice assists educational policy makers and college and university administrators, faculty, and staff to enhance the conditions for student success. However, as we reflected on the DEEP findings we concluded that they serve as important principles for contemporary student affairs practice. This prospect actually captured our attention early in the course of the research project as it seemed that the 20 DEEP schools had unique, nontraditional approaches to student affairs. Our work in this volume uses the richness of the DEEP data and findings as a means to consider and outline innovative models for student affairs practice from a student engagement and success point of view.

Educationally Effective Practice and Models for Student Affairs

In the chapters that follow, we elaborate on ways to organize student affairs for student engagement and success. We begin our consideration of educationally effective models for student affairs practice with a discussion of six traditional models generated through analysis of the student affairs literature: extracurricular, functional silos, student services, co-curricular, seamless learning, and competitive/adversarial models. Following the discussion of the traditional models, we then introduce five innovative models that grew out of the DEEP research: student-centered ethic of care, student-driven, student agency, academic/ student affairs collaboration, and academic-centered. In addition to the

DEEP findings and student affairs literature, these models are based on our combined experience as instructors in student affairs preparation programs, researchers in higher education, and student affairs professionals.

We learned through the DEEP research and demonstrate in this text is that there is more than one way to practice student affairs. In fact, we hope that this book opens up a long-term conversation about the many potential models of student affairs practice. Most importantly, from the DEEP research came the insight that the nature and mission of student affairs on these campuses was tailored to meet the student's needs, fit with the culture and mission of the campus, and focus on student learning. There is no magic organizational model for student affairs practice. Rather, careful consideration of the campus culture, hard work, thoughtful reflection, and a clear understanding of how student affairs can facilitate student success are essential ingredients in developing student affairs organizations that truly are effective. Come with us now, as we consider the student affairs organizations models we encountered on our tour of DEEP institutions.

PART II

TRADITIONAL MODELS OF STUDENT AFFAIRS DEPARTMENTS AND DIVISIONS

CHAPTER 3

OUT-OF-CLASSROOM-CENTERED ESTABLISHED MODELS

Entering the student center, one is struck by the vibrant colors of the student organization banners hanging from the ceiling. It is obvious from the banners advertising clubs' and organizations' events as well as the din from students milling around that extracurricular activities abound at this institution. Student leaders often exclaim that they learn more out of the classroom than they do in it. This point of view is proudly backed up with the conviction that "no one checks your GPA after you graduate. But everyone looks at your resume for leadership, involvement, and out-of-classroom experience." The student activities office has an elaborate system of student leadership. The most coveted positions include orientation leaders, student ambassadors, and resident assistants. Students vehemently state that they would undertake these positions whether or not they were paid. The life-skills experience, sense of achievement, and fun gained, they state, is its own reward. As expressed by one student, "This is what college is all about." A stroll through the student center gives one the impression that this space is dedicated to students. While an occasional faculty member grabs a cup of coffee or light meal, few faculty and students sit at the tables strewn around the atrium. Faculty state that the student center "is a place for the students. We do most of our interaction with students in the classroom or in our offices. It works fine. They have a space where they can pursue their activities, and we have our space where we pursue the academic mission of the institution."

In 1931, Robert C. Clothier made a measured plea for educators to develop a personnel function within higher education institutions. The recommended definition of this proposed area was:

Personnel work in a college or university is the systematic bringing to bear on the individual student all those influences, of whatever nature, which will stimulate him [*sic*] and assist him, through his own efforts, to develop in body, mind and character to the limit of his individual capacity for growth, and helping him to apply his powers so developed most effectively to the work of the world. (p. 10)

This early statement of student personnel work, similar to those quoted below, made no reference to this work occurring solely in or out of the classroom environment. In fact, all members of the college community (e.g., "professor, instructor, dean, registrar, adviser, coach, proctor, yes even janitor" [p. 10]) were called upon to perform the roles of student personnel. "*Student affairs* refers to the administrative unit on a college campus responsible for those out-of-classroom staff members, programs, functions, and services that contribute to the education and development of students" (Javinar, 2000, p. 85).

Despite the early calls for student personnel work (later called *student affairs*) to occur throughout the institution, the model of student affairs work that emerged was an extracurricular or out-of-classroom approach. "The particular province of the student personnel concern was the *extra*curricular. Extra in this instance meaning not only *outside of* or *beyond*, but to many *peripheral* and *unnecessary*" (Brown,

1972, p. 42). Rather than a true emphasis on the whole student, the emphasis has been on the psychosocial experiences of students (Nuss, 2003). In residence halls, campus activities, or recreation, student affairs–sponsored programs, services, and policies were supportive of the academic functions of higher education (NASPA, 1989). As early as 1937, *The Student Personnel Point of View* (ACE) delineated functions of student affairs. Looking at this list, many or most of the suggested activities (e.g., supervision of extracurricular activities, development of religious life activities, coordination of financial aid, provision of food service, administration of student discipline, and assistance to students trying to clarify purposes) take place in an out-of-classroom environment.

This chapter delineates the history and philosophical and theoretical underpinnings of the extracurricular model, a traditional model in student affairs administration. In particular, the strengths and weaknesses of this model are discussed to situate it in past, current, and future student affairs practice. Underscored by a predominantly social student development approach, the extracurricular model is based on an assumption of separate student affairs and academic affairs missions, functions, and pedagogies. With limited or no overlap with academic affairs, "institutional factors and conditions work together in different colleges and universities to promote learning and personal development through out-of-class learning experiences" (Kuh et al., 1991, p. 4).

The Extracurricular Life of the Campus

"For years student personnel workers have identified themselves as educators who are concerned about the total student and whose role involves primarily the out-of-class activities" (Brown, 1972, p. 42). What would a campus that embraces the extracurricular model of student affairs practice look like? What programs would be sponsored? What activities would students participate in? Throughout this chapter, illustrations of the extracurricular model will be offered through vignettes outlining examples of programs, policies, and organizational structures of student affairs. These vignettes are set apart from the remainder of the chapter text through the use of italics. The accounts and names in these vignettes are, of course, fictitious.

> *High Involvement College (HIC) has a well-developed student affairs division. Well-versed in student affairs practice, the staff of HIC has spent years expanding and developing a wide range of out-of-classroom experiences. While some of these, for example, community service opportunities, share similar learning goals (e.g., development of critical thinking) to in-class experiences, the majority of student affairs–sponsored programs are not academically focused. The offices housed under the Division of Student Affairs include career development, student activities, orientation, community service, student center, residential life, athletics, and judicial affairs. Bridges between the student affairs staff and faculty members are tenuous. Each year, a concerted effort is made to involve faculty in campus life. These efforts include attempts to recruit student organization advisors, orientation participants, and residential life living-learning sponsors. But, on the whole, faculty sees its role as separate and distinct from the out-of-classroom mission espoused by the student affairs division.*

In retrospect, today's student affairs educators may wonder at the choice to split in- and out-of-classroom learning. With the current emphasis on seamless student learning (ACPA, 1996), such a strict separation may seem ill advised. But, as discussed in chapter 1, there were and are many reasons to organize student and academic affairs as separate entities. Advantages accrued to student affairs as a result of an extracurricular approach occurred because the model:

1. Allows specialized expertise in the functional areas of career development, student activities, residence life, and union management, among others, to be developed.
2. Encourages discrete budgeting and resources to develop within student affairs divisions.
3. Frees faculty to concentrate their efforts on teaching, research, and service.
4. Permits the expansion of programs, services, and policies that would, most likely, have remained underdeveloped if integrated closely with academic affairs.

5. Creates the opportunity for institutions to expand learning, leadership, and developmental opportunities for students beyond academics.

Despite any strengths or weaknesses of the extracurricular model, this early model of student affairs practice established a medium in which student affairs practitioners constructed a rich array of student-centered opportunities. Using the extracurricular model, student affairs professionals have

> infinite settings outside the classroom which provide the student with opportunities to clarify values and purposes, confront ideas, emotions, and issues, bring new information to bear upon situations or new ways to organize information, accept the consequences of behavior, and grow in ability to lead and relate to others. (Appleton, Briggs, & Rhatigan, 1978, p. 47)

Philosophy of the Extracurricular Model

Rhatigan (2003) speculated that the impetus for a model of extracurricular services and programs originated with the 1937 *Student Personnel Point of View* (ACE, 1937). "By outlining so many separate services, they [the 1937 authors] failed to see how this would affect relationships with other divisions and how specialization would undercut the idea of wholeness central to the espoused philosophy" (p. 17). Cognitive development occurred within the classroom through individualized study, writing, reading, and activities related to critical thinking and the development of liberally educated citizens (Bloland, Stamatakos, & Rogers, 1994). Social, emotional, and noncognitive development occurred out of the classroom through club and organization involvement, leadership development, campus employment, program development, and environmental management, among others.

The extracurricular model provided significant saliency for the student affairs field. The possibility of out-of-classroom experiences creates a teaching and learning medium in which to promote a wide variety of knowledge, skills, and perspectives. In such settings, students are exposed to diverse populations of people, learn management and leadership, work collaboratively with peers, articulate a point of view to institutional leadership, and gain confidence and expertise.

Student organizations that offer opportunities for applying knowledge to real situations such as defining and pursuing common goals, preparing for and meeting financial obligations, participating in democratic decision making, and contributing to conflict resolution reflect a pragmatic approach to learning. Student affairs efforts such as career development, counseling, student activities, living-learning environments, student government, and leadership training reflect directly a philosophy of pragmatism in that students are openly encouraged and supported to gain understanding by using and applying knowledge (Knock, 1988, p. 15).

The rich and varied campus life of HIC is a draw for prospective students. While academic goals are important, the presence of world-class performing arts, scholarly and popular lectures, annual campuswide weekend celebrations (often centered around major athletic events), and major concerts builds a rich campus community. Furthermore, the services offered through career development workshops and offerings, enrollment-management gains achieved through orientation, and the student responsibility taught through the judicial program have long-lasting educational effects. Extending beyond the campus walls, a policy of reduced admission for community members enriches the local environment as well.

History and Characteristics of the Extracurricular Model

The extracurricular model did not originate with the founding mothers and fathers of the student affairs field. It was invented by students.

Student life and the activities of students in the colonial colleges were dominated by religious activity, a strict moralistic discipline, and a classical curriculum. . . . From the mid-eighteenth century to the mid-nineteenth century, literary clubs and debating societies were the common form of organized student activities. Students had found that the classical curriculum did not provide a means of discussing the political and social issues of the time and established these groups as a supplement to the curriculum. (Saddlemire, 1988, p. 262)

The literary societies evolved into judicial bodies, Greek organizations, debate clubs, and campus publications. Social fraternities, founded in 1825, would expand as a system to include sororities and provide housing (Nuss, 2003). As such, the personnel and services function of early higher education was established outside the confines of the curriculum and academic mission of higher education institutions. With the establishment of the first student union at University of Pennsylvania in 1901 (Saddlemire, 1988), out-of-classroom activities under the purview of administrators were clearly established. This focused interest in out-of-class learning progressed through the 1960s and 1970s as the student affairs field grew.

At HIC, student affairs practice primarily occurs in the residence halls, student unions, athletic fields, and other nonacademic-based facilities and locations. Similar to the earliest student affairs professionals, HIC student affairs staff take advantage of the rich out-of-classroom learning opportunities by developing leadership development programs, student activities, and structured student staffing patterns. Clubs and organizations are an excellent venue to teach leadership skills. Student government, Greek organizations, recreational clubs, and ethnic affinity groups provide a medium in which students experience working collaboratively, gain new knowledge, practice unfamiliar skills, and interact with persons different from themselves. HIC has a wide range of leadership offerings: leadership retreats, organization officer training sessions, a resource library, a speaker series for organizational leaders, and a wide variety of leadership opportunities. Student affairs staff have proposed a leadership minor to be taught by their staff, but faculty have rejected the proposal as not being academically focused.

Theoretical Foundations of the Extracurricular Model

The extracurricular model rests on a foundation of psychosocial student development and leadership theory. The evolution of student personnel workers as educators provided an opportunity for a unique theoretical perspective, student development, to define the work of student affairs practitioners. This approach had particular saliency for out-of-classroom learning situations.

Reliance on Psychosocial Student Development Models. The underlying theoretical perspective for the extracurricular model is the psychosocial student development theories. Chickering (1969) and Gilligan (1982) are developmental theorists who offer particular theoretical efficacy to this approach. Each of Chickering's (1969) seven vectors (i.e., developing competence, managing emotions, moving through autonomy toward interdependence, developing mature interpersonal relationships, establishing identity, developing purpose, and developing integrity) (Chickering & Reisser, 1993) informs programs, services, policy, and environment management within the extracurricular student affairs model. Using Chickering's model, student activities are not simply ways to entertain students but a means to develop their social competence and identity development. On-campus student employment is not inexpensive staff coverage but a vehicle through which students develop purpose and integrity. Discipline procedures need not be a punitive means to control students but a way to challenge students about maturity and interdependence.

Residence life settings are particularly apt locations in which to pursue extracurricular goals. Students who have never shared a room live in close proximity to another person. Idiosyncrasies, personal values, and habits are all up for negotiation and discussion in such a close environment. Students who serve as residence assistants and paraprofessional staff learn significant lessons about themselves and others as they counsel students about personal issues, help their peers negotiate the campus environment, and respond to crises. In the extracurricular model, residence halls are often considered "off limits" by faculty and nonresidence staff. Students, on the other hand, call these facilities "home." They make connections to a community, which results in lasting relationships. The satisfaction (or lack of satisfaction) they find in this environment profoundly shapes their college experience.

Written from a female psychosocial perspective, Gilligan's (1982) theory provides theoretical strength to the extracurricular model. Her ideas concerning the primacy of relationship building give direction for social and emotional development for students as well as for professional collegiality and development among student affairs professionals. The interpersonally rich field of student affairs has gained significantly from

Gilligan's theory about the role of relationships in human development. Residence hall living, using Gilligan's theory, can be organized around perspectives about the limits of responsibility to others. Student behavior can be understood in the context of possible choices about relationship building or autonomy. Gilligan opened the door for student affairs professionals to embrace relationship-oriented development models of mattering and marginality (Schlossberg, 1989). These models provide theoretical efficacy for understanding development in the relationship-rich out-of-classroom context.

Leadership Development. The development of students' leadership skills and aptitude is a major purpose of the extracurricular model approach to student affairs. When students serve as paraprofessionals in the residence halls, orientation programs, or career development assistants; attend leadership retreats and workshops; and obtain advisement through their leadership roles in clubs and organizations, leadership is taught. This leadership is linked developmentally to the growth of democratic values, citizenship, and commitment to community (Hamrick, Evans, & Schuh, 2002).

Breen (1970) conducted one of the first published surveys of campus leadership programs. His study found that successful programs (a) involved students in the planning, (b) involved the student activities office in a major role, (c) employed weekend retreats as a popular model, and (d) utilized group work and experience-based learning models. Subsequent surveys and research on leadership programs confirmed the heavy involvement of student activities offices in these efforts. The skills, attitudes, and approaches taught through these early leadership efforts still have current relevance, but recent models such as servant leadership, moral leadership, and collaborative leadership (Komives, Lucas, & McMahon, 1998) place an emphasis on relationship, ethics, and civic development rather than simply task accomplishment or leadership skill attainment.

> *When a student leader at HIC is asked how she manages her time, she may admit that it is a struggle. A student leaders' weekly schedule can typically involve 12 to 15 meetings per week of out-of-classroom involvement. Leaders may be compelled to skip an occasional class for important*

meeting with the president or the provost. Faculty, when urged to excuse a student leader, may have mixed feelings about students who are asked, by college administrators, to split their time and focus between in- and out-of-classroom activities. Faculty priorities for students may include academic excellence, graduate study, or research. Extracurricular involvement may appear to be a frivolous add-on. Student leaders, on the other hand, believe that out-of-classroom experience will yield the best results in terms of future career plans.

The extracurricular model embodies the assumptions that (1) student engagement is initiated by student affairs professionals; (2) faculty emphasize intellectual, not social, development; and (3) organizational configurations define the separate nature of student and academic affairs.

Student Engagement Initiated by Student Affairs Professionals. In the extracurricular model, student affairs staff are responsible for the choices made about the services, programs, and environment molded to advance student engagement. For example, despite the use of students as staff members and the development rationale upon which such practice is built, the staffing patterns determined, policies enacted, and best practices employed in the extracurricular model originate with student affairs professionals. While students are often recruited as para- and semiprofessional staff members, the framework, procedures, and overall direction of the engagement achieved is managed by full-time staff.

The limits and details of this staff-centered approach to student affairs practice have been debated and refined over the years. Its essentials can be illustrated through several longstanding debates within the student affairs field. Should student club and organization advising be direct or indirect? Should students have the right to determine community standards or are there minimal standards, particularly in the residence halls (e.g., quiet hours, alcohol use) that should serve as a foundation upon which further standards are then built by students? If student affairs professionals are more mature, experienced, and knowledgeable about educational practice, should not they make decisions in the best interests of students? Student affairs professionals wrestle each day with questions about responsibilities to be shared (and not shared) with students, the limits of standards of practice, and nuances of their role with students.

Organizational Configurations for the Extracurricular Model

Higher education institutions have been described as dualistically organized into a hierarchy among administrators and collegium among faculty (see Table 3.1) (Alpert, 1986; Birnbaum, 1991). This dualistic structure is amplified in the Extracurricular Model as different cultures, ways of operating, and standards of practice are employed for student affairs administrators and faculty.

The hierarchy or administrative "side" of the institution is characterized by standardization, routinization, and coordination. The collegial faculty and academic "side" of the institution uses consensus decision making, assumes leadership as first among equals, and recognizes expert authority. Applying these ideas to the extracurricular model, college life can be divided into the social out-of-class (hierarchy) and intellectual classroom (collegium). The existence of these two disparate organizational forms interferes with attempts to integrate student learning goals throughout the institution. Faculty speak a different language than administrators. Communication between the two groups follows contradictory norms of practice. The goals for both "sides" are different—sometimes conflicting. This dualistic structure creates a circumstance where distinct in- and out-of-classroom goals and practices emerge. College community members belonging to these different organization structures in the same institution often disagree about the importance of out-of-classroom involvement, the role of the

Table 3.1 Dualistic Model of Higher Education Organization

Bureaucratic Model	Collegial Model
Interrelated to others	Autonomous
Centralized authority	Decentralized authority
Set organizational goals and maintain standards of performance	Produce, apply, preserve, and communicate knowledge
Need to change institution in times of retrenchment	Resistant to institutional change
Demand for measurable product	Cannot measure product
Nontenured	Tenured

extracurricular functions, and the language with which one describes college life.

With the presence of these two vastly different organizational approaches, it is no mystery that the extracurricular model developed as a separate entity to the academic purposes and goals. A flaw in viewing the institution this way is that students experience the college more holistically than the dramatic separation of the curricular and extracurricular assumed by faculty and staff (Kuh et al., 1991). A second flaw in this dualistic approach is represented in the quantum organizational theories of Wheatley (1994) and Zohar (1997). Wheatley "stresses the need to see things *in their wholeness* [italics added] rather than in ever-narrowing parts if one seeks to understand and influence future organizations" (as cited in Rhatigan, 2003, pp. 20–21). Quantum models of organizational theory emphasize connection, dynamism, collaboration, and attention to the whole. Allen and Cherrey (2000) linked these quantum approaches to organizational theory to student affairs practice. Living and working in a quantum, postmodern institution requires

> that student affairs professionals bring their talents to the table, make necessary changes in their practice, develop new capacities, challenge traditional ways of working and develop the new relationships needed to influence institutional leadership and transformation. To do so, we need to develop new ways of relating, influencing change, learning, and leading. (p. 22)

The future of organizational functioning is in wholeness. Brown (1972) previewed this holistic approach to organization and practice in general.

> It is time for student personnel workers to recognize that they too have been dealing with only a part of the student, and it is no more valid for them to expect effectiveness in dealing with the student's development, independent of his [*sic*] academic life, than it is for the professor to think a student's personal self does not affect his academic growth. (p. 38)

The debate about organizational effectiveness and structural ways to achieve high-quality student affairs practice has expressed itself in the reporting options for VPSAs and deans of students. (For ease in discussion, only the VPSA will be used in the examples.) At the institutional level, two primary organizational configurations have been used by higher education administrators to organize and determine the reporting structures for divisions and departments of student affairs. These are (a) student affairs as an independent division reporting to the president (Figure 3.1) and (b) student affairs as a subdivision of academic affairs (Figure 3.2).

Student Affairs as an Independent Division
In the first model, the VPSA is equal to other institutional executive officers including those in development, finance, administration,

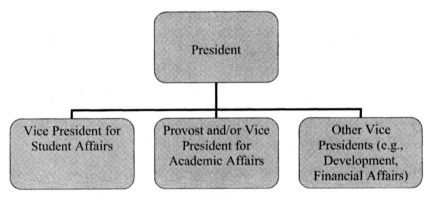

Figure 3.1 Student Affairs as an Independent Division.

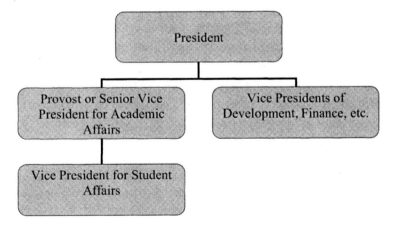

Figure 3.2 Student Affairs as an Entity of Academic Affairs

and academics (although, as Sandeen [1991] notes, the academic vice president is often "first among equals"). The benefits of this direct reporting structure include (1) recognition of the equal importance of student and academic affairs; (2) an independent budget and resource allocation; (3) opportunity to advocate for student affairs programs and policies directly to the president; and (4) inclusion on the president's staff and, hence, institution-wide decision making.

Student affairs as a detached and independent division, as represented by the first model, existed at only one of the 20 DEEP schools investigated. As described in the report of campus visits at that institution

> This puts the VPSA at the table every week with the academic chairs. Such regular interaction maintains a strong relationship and continuing dialogue between the chairs and the student affairs division and has led to a high degree of faculty involvement in student affairs programs. (NSSE, 2003e, p. 9)

The existence of this configuration at a DEEP school points to its saliency. But the fact that the majority of DEEP institutions had a structure where the VPSA reported to the provost points to the possible academic/student affairs links in the second model.

Student Affairs Reporting to the Provost

The second predominant student affairs reporting model is to the senior academic affairs officer. The benefits of this model include (1) more opportunities for collaboration between the student and academic affairs missions, (2) less competition between the academic and student affairs resource structures, and (3) potential buy-in by the academic officer into the student affairs mission. In discussing the role of the senior student affairs officer (called "chief student affairs officer" [CSAO] in his lexicon), Sandeen (1991) points to the importance of the senior student affairs–senior academic affairs officer relationship.

> The CSAO's relationship to the chief academic officer is almost as important as the relationship to the president. If the CSAO and the chief academic officer have widely differing views about education and the role of the university in its relations with students, the separation between academic and student life will most likely be

great . . . the goal of the CSAO-chief academic officer relationship should be ... working together for the education of students, so that the college experience is viewed as a whole. . . . Very little will be accomplished if the CSAO attempts to compete with the chief academic officer, or is not supportive of the major academic goals of the institution. Most important, both academic leaders need each other and can improve the institution's educational program by working together. (pp. 27–29)

Although debates about the efficacy of these two models exist in the student affairs field, there are clearly strengths and weaknesses to both. The appropriateness of the model depends on institutional history, administrators' personalities, institutional context and characteristics, and the goals sought within the institution. There can be no generalized advice given about the "best" way to achieve the VPSA reporting structure.

Sandeen argues the same theme that emerged from the DEEP research. Regardless of the direct or indirect presidential reporting structure, student affairs officers should not advocate for a separate out-of-classroom curriculum. This latter approach mitigates attempts to integrate the academic and student affairs missions and undermines the whole student philosophy.

Themes From DEEP Research

While the DEEP research discussed in this book found that there are many means to achieve student engagement (Kuh et al., 2005), none of the institutions studied exhibited the Extracurricular Model. In fact, a significant finding of the DEEP research was that faculty and administrators (including student affairs professionals) within these institutions took a holistic, collaborative approach to student engagement. The activities leading to student engagement and success were not sharply divided into the in- and out-of-classroom realms. Rather, engagement was viewed as an institutional commitment in which all were involved. Assumptions about territory and role were reduced in favor of working collaboratively toward student success.

Student engagement has two key components that contribute to student success. The first is the amount of time and effort students put into their studies and other activities that lead to the experiences and outcomes that constitute student success. The second is the ways the institution allocates resources and organizes learning opportunities and services to induce students to participate in and benefit from such activities (Kuh et al., 2005, p. 9).

Notably, this definition does not split educationally purposeful activities into the in- and out-of-classroom realms. The models discussed earlier speak to this collaboration.

Strengths and Successful Strategies Within the Extracurricular Model

The strengths of the extracurricular model were discussed earlier in the chapter. Several points are briefly reiterated here prior to a more in-depth discussion of the weaknesses of the model.

The extracurricular model, though perhaps out of date with today's emphasis on student and academic affairs collaboration (ACPA, 1996), has served the field well. It enabled student affairs professionals to create a wide range of educational opportunities. Several areas of student affairs administration have thrived under the extracurricular model. These include student activities and residence life (particularly in the areas of community building and social programming). Extracurricular involvement has been repeatedly related to retention, satisfaction with the institution, and academic gains (Astin, 1993; Woo & Bilynsky, 1994). Tinto's (1993) model of retention paid particular attention to students' extracurricular lives in his discussion of social integration. The leadership development resulting from the volunteer and paid student leader opportunities as a result of the practices within the extracurricular model has been substantial.

Orientation, service learning, academic advising, and career development, areas more closely aligned with the academic mission, fit less well structurally and philosophically with the extracurricular model.

Significant gains in student satisfaction with his or her institution as well as increased retention percentages have long been associated with the out-of-classroom activities and development associated with the extracurricular model. The emphasis on community building has benefited higher education institutions by engendering more relationship-oriented, collaborative, and other-oriented environments.

And, one cannot begin to count the gains resulting from the leadership skills, knowledge, and experience taught in out-of-classroom circumstances. Additionally, the extracurricular model involves a concentrated effort on community building. Proponents of the model presume that healthy communities are an essential aspect of campus life. Residence halls, clubs and organizations, commuter programs, and any affiliation-building activities are a way to achieve this community.

Weaknesses Within the Extracurricular Model

Despite the successes of the extracurricular model, particularly in the formative years of the student affairs field, several weaknesses illustrate the fact that this approach may need to be replaced with more current models. These weaknesses include the lack of integration of the student affairs and academic missions, a bifurcation of the whole student philosophy, inability to achieve the whole person goal, failure to serve all students, and confusion about the purpose of college.

Lack of Integration. "Higher education took the wrong fork in the road when it thrust personnel maintenance upon staff with specialized duties" (Brown, 1972, p. 37). Among the first to encourage student affairs staff to move student affairs efforts from the extracurricular to the curricular, Brown challenged the out-of-classroom approach to student affairs practice. His challenge was echoed by the authors of the 1989 *A Perspective on Student Affairs* (NASPA, 1989). "The Academic Mission of the Institution is Preeminent. . . . The work of student affairs should not compete with and cannot substitute for the academic experience. As a partner in the educational enterprise, student affairs enhances and supports the academic mission" (NASPA, 1989, p. 12). Although seen by some as relegating student affairs to a subordinate position, this sentiment called for collaboration and integration of the student affairs and academic missions, a sentiment advocated again in *The Student Learning Imperative* (ACPA, 1996).

In the formative days of the student affairs field, debates raged about the importance of the student affairs mission compared to academic affairs. Many complained that student affairs professionals were often treated as second-class citizens. Their mission, argued some, was as educationally valuable as—and, therefore, equal to—the academic mission of the curriculum and in-classroom efforts. Regardless of one's individual stance in this debate, it is clear that the extracurricular model does not outline a clearly delineated role for faculty. All parties in the process—students, student affairs professionals, and faculty—struggle to envision a role for faculty in the social and emotional development goals of this model.

Inability to Achieve a Whole Student Philosophy Goal. The extracurricular model has a fundamental flaw as an approach to working with students. The out-of-classroom venue in which its educational goals are achieved is not amenable to all students. The model works extremely well for students at both ends of the disciplinary continuum: student leaders who are extremely involved or students who are frequent visitors to the disciplinary system. Both groups of students receive a significant amount of time and attention from student affairs staff. But "what about the more typical student who never sees a counselor, who never creates a disturbance in the residence hall, or who is never a campus leader? His [sic] contact with the student personnel staff is limited and his life style is affected very indirectly, if at all, by student personnel services or policies" (Brown, 1972, p. 37). Surely the founders and early theorists of the student affairs field had a broader approach for the field in mind.

The predominantly one-on-one approach of the extracurricular model precludes any staff member's ability to have an impact on all students. While all may be influenced, at some point, by a program, policy, or approach to student development, a disproportionate amount of staff time is spent with student leaders and students requiring disciplinary intervention. Brown, as early as 1972, noted this weakness: "One of the major weaknesses of current student development programs and student affairs functions is that they directly affect a small minority of students and even indirectly have almost no impact on the academic aspects of student life" (p. 43). Recent technological interventions have mitigated some of this overemphasis on too few students, but the flaw in the model remains.

Confusion About College Purposes. Student affairs professionals working with students who are actively (and perhaps overly) involved in the extracurricular life of the campus have often challenged them to maintain a balance. Too often, the out-of-classroom activities, leadership positions, and learning priorities can be, particularly for young students, more interesting and appealing than studying, taking examinations, and completing academic assignments. As such, students may lose perspective about the importance of their academic goals. When the extracurricular becomes more important than the curricular, the purpose of college is lost. This is the case for students as much as for student affairs professionals. The extracurricular model, with its emphasis on social and emotional development, inherently more interesting for many than intellectual development, is fundamentally prone to this type of misunderstanding. Student affairs professionals, students, and faculty would have to collaborate closely about the ultimate goals of higher education in order to avoid this confusion.

Summary

Since the colonial colleges higher education has been a 24-hour a day operation. Students live on campus, eat in campus facilities, exercise in college-owned buildings, and study at all hours of the day and night in college-owned spaces. While the expectations of service have long been present, the assumption of learning goals underscoring these services has not always been assumed. One could argue that the introduction of the student learning approach to student affairs is the death knell for the extracurricular model. If seamless learning is the goal, then there is no in- and out-of-classroom. All campus environments are ripe for every possible type of student learning and development. Data from the DEEP research show that institutions with high engagement and graduation rates experience no clear-cut separation between in- and out-of-classroom learning. Faculty and student affairs staff see their roles as collaborative and serving the goal of student learning.

The connection between the extracurricular model and student learning, though perhaps obvious to some, is not without difficulties. A basic premise of the extracurricular model, at least as it has been practiced in the past, is the separation of social/emotional and cognitive learning. While learning in the social/emotional realm is certainly of value, the primary purpose of higher education is the academic (or cognitive development) mission. This difference between the primacy of cognitive development and secondary nature of social/emotional development has been the source of much discussion about second-class citizenship in student affairs. Discussion about student learning has led to confusion about the need for student affairs practitioners to teach in a classroom setting and, conversely, for faculty to teach in an out-of-classroom setting.

With the tide of accepted practice moving away from an extracurricular approach, why would an institution choose to employ this model? As with all approaches discussed in this book, the institution's context, history, and educational goals dictate the fit of any model to the particular setting. The following questions may guide an assessment of the fit of the extracurricular model to current institutional needs:

- What is the nature of the academic and student affairs missions? Are they separate entities? Is there a desire to integrate the academic and student affairs missions?
- What is the philosophy of the student affairs professionals regarding practice? Do they see themselves as educators, administrators, or development specialists?
- What is the nature of the student body? Do they come to the institution expressly to develop leadership and other skills in an out-of-classroom context?
- How interested are the faculty in the out-of-classroom life of the students? How interested are student affairs professionals in the in-classroom life of students? Is there any room for collaboration between these two groups?
- Do any of the institutional characteristics (e.g., size, complexity, history) preclude close collaboration between academic and student affairs goals? Are the goals of both better achieved through a distinct separation of task and mission?

The answers to these questions can assist higher education administrators as they determine the model of organizational practice that best suits the needs of their institutions. In any case, there is more than one way to organize student affairs.

CHAPTER 4

ADMINISTRATIVE-CENTERED
ESTABLISHED MODELS

The VPSA takes great pride in the Division of Student Affairs she built. Established on a firm foundation of organizational theory, management principles, and leadership ideas, the Division of Student Affairs is an institutional example of administrative efficiency. While the educational background and training of the VPSA includes student development and counseling, her professional philosophy leans toward student services. A veteran of the student affairs profession, the VPSA knows that the words "student development" do not sell well at the executive leadership level of her institution. Retention, fiscal responsibility, and strategic planning are management realities in her world.

Over time, the practice of student affairs administration has evolved with two approaches: One of service and the other of development. The former approach is concerned with the efficient delivery of programs and services to meet an array of student needs, whereas the latter is concerned with the purposeful design of programs and services to effect desired student outcomes. (Javinar, 2000, p. 86)

History and Background of Models

The student affairs field grew out of the twin purposes of student guidance (i.e., discipline and *in loco parentis*) and administrative need (Appleton et al., 1978). The two approaches have taken divergent paths, particularly as student affairs functions were interpreted by different institutions. Institutions adopting a student services approach can use an administrative perspective as the logic for organizing programs and functions. Student development models and theories may be an aspect of the organizing philosophy, yet the predominant influence is administrative principles, leadership, and management. In contrast, institutions adopting a student development approach use counseling and human development as their foundation.

This chapter discusses administrative-centered approaches to student affairs practice. The two models discussed here, Functional Silos and Student Services, place the administrative perspective (as contrasted to a student-centered approach) at the center of student affairs practice. It is not that these models fail to serve students. They simply organize their functions and approaches from an organizational, leadership, or management perspective rather than student development.

Student affairs folklore, right or wrong, supports the belief that institutional size, in particular, dictates whether the student affairs division staff takes an administrative-centered or student-centered approach to student affairs practice. In other words, large institutions are more administratively oriented while smaller institutions are more student oriented. We argue here that the administrative-centered model, similar to others discussed in this book, is not determined by institutional type but rather by the unique characteristics of the institution, historical approaches to student affairs practice at the specific institution, and leadership priorities of the administration. In other words, the character of the institution will determine the philosophical perspective driving the model of student affairs practice employed. This book purports the belief that any model of student affairs practice needs to be congruent with the institutional mission. Therefore, some institutions are more suited to administrative-oriented student affairs practice while others are more suited to a development-oriented student affairs practice. Without getting into "right" or "wrong" and "better" or "worse," this chapter discusses student affairs models for practice, which are more administratively focused, including two prominent models: functional silos and student services.

The reader may feel that we are splitting a hair by describing these two models in a separate manner. In fact, professionals would be hard pressed to find an institution that has any of the models described in this book in a "pure" form. Student affairs practice is often, if not always, a hybrid or combination of different models. For the sake of defining and seeking to understand the different approaches to student affairs practice, we describe the models in a more definitive form than anyone might observe in the field. In fact, the models described here are almost caricatures of what one would actually find in the field.

Bureaucracy as the Underpinning Structure for Administrative-Centered Approaches

Administrators have a wide variety of organizational theories and models to use to understand and guide their educational practice. Education organizational theorists (see Birnbaum, 1991; Bolman & Deal, 2003) place organizational theories into four broad categories: bureaucratic, cultural, political, and systemic. The administrative-oriented model uses the bureaucratic model as a guide for its organization.

The bureaucratic theory first advanced by Weber (1947) is, by far, the most prevalent theory of organizational structure in the Western world. Higher education organizations certainly use the bureaucratic model more than any other, although many (Baldridge, Curtis, Ecker, & Riley, 1980; Cohen & March, 1986) hold that the political model is a more salient lens through which to understand colleges and universities. Every administrator, every student for that matter, with varying levels of success, knows how to negotiate the bureaucracy. Students bemoan it as "red tape," administrators skilled at its standards of communication know how to "get things done," the politically astute know how to perform end runs around bureaucratic protocols. Although most of us dislike bureaucracy, its logic provides a philosophy and organizational framework upon which student affairs work can be achieved. Bureaucracies embody particular tensions that exist within student affairs and administrative practice.

Specialization and Fragmentation Versus Integration

Bureaucracies by definition are organizations where functions are specialized (Morgan, 1997). Offices are created to serve particular purposes. Job descriptions are written to delineate responsibilities of staff. As bureaucracies become more mature, their functions are increasingly specialized; some say "fossilized." This inherent specialization tendency of bureaucracy leads to red tape, which occurs when offices fail to coordinate their functions and send students from one place to another. When red tape abounds, services offered through various offices do not overlap and communication is limited or nonexistent. Despite any relationship between functions, offices perform their functions as if they are discrete entities—separate silos, so to speak.

Although specialization is a major force within bureaucracies, integration of functions is equally important. Integration is largely achieved through coordination. Some of the ways coordination is achieved are socialization, communication, cultural artifacts, standard operating procedures, and planning. In a classic bureaucracy, coordination is achieved through the chain of command and supervisory mechanisms, as a function of group and individual meetings, and through communication structures that inform organizational members of each other's behavior (Blau, 1970/1973; Simon, 1957; Weber, 1947).

Student affairs has a unique history concerning coordination. In the field's original founding document, *The Student Personnel Point of View* (ACE, 1937), coordination was prominently discussed. In a publication limited in size, the authors dedicated a large number of words and pages to the importance of student services' functions coordination. The coordination and specialization focus in both the 1937 and 1949 versions of *The Student Personnel Point of View* (ACE, 1937, 1949) may have led subsequent student affairs theorists' and practitioners' emphasis on bureaucracy as an organizing principle for their work. Several original textbooks in the student affairs field, *Student Services: A Handbook for the Profession* (Delworth & Hanson, 1980, 1989) and *Student Affairs Functions in Higher Education* (Rentz & Saddlemire, 1988) delineate the functions of student affairs by area and topic. As such, these early student affairs textbooks adopted a specialized approach to student affairs practice. The danger in this approach is the fragmentation that results when people think of their functional areas as separate, rather than related, areas of service for students. Through specialization, functions become more isolated and independent. Through coordination, administrators connect the functions through congruent goals, practices, or ways the services and programs are used.

Public Versus Private

The urge toward specialization and the split between different parts of the institution are not so different from the public/private split sometimes sought within organizational life. The personal has always been associated with feminine characteristics and the public with masculine (Harding, 1987, 1991). Feminist theorists have often argued that women need to occupy the public domain as well as dismantle the barriers to thinking that the personal does not belong within the public. In fact, the rallying cry, "the personal is political," raised by feminists in the 1980s makes the point that a separation between public and private is arbitrary and inaccurate. The public/private split is one worthy of exploration and thought in student affairs, a profession long relegated to or celebrated as (depending on your perspective) feminine. The dominance of women in educational fields certainly is reflected in student affairs where, at least at the nonexecutive level of administration, women outnumber men by a significant percentage.

Professionals in the student affairs field have long interchanged the personal and public. We work with students on issues that are clearly private in nature: health, families, and relationships, among others. The University of Maine at Farmington, a DEEP project institution,

> has fostered an environment that actively supports the mixing of personal and work lives in healthy ways. Students encounter their professors on a regular basis in this small community; thus, they

have many opportunities for informal conversations. These frequent contacts also help to reinforce students' identities in the minds of faculty. (NSSE, 2003g, p. 43)

With the longstanding overlap of personal and public, it is not at all surprising that one way student affairs administrators managed this tension was to establish two models for practice: administrative and counseling/developmental.

Centralization Versus Decentralization

In addition to the bureaucratic tendency to specialize and fragment, a structural tension in bureaucratic structures is centralization versus decentralization. In theory, bureaucracies seek to centralize functions. If you imagine the standard pyramid style organizational chart, the impression given is that the person at the top is "in charge" (see Figure 4.1).

As the person to whom the entire division ultimately reports, one may have the impression that this "top" person is privy to all communication and knowledge available. This perception is often displayed on campus during a crisis (for example, an athletic scandal). Vice presidents experiencing this kind of crisis may be fired or forced to resign as trustees, students, parents, and local community members state that he or she "should have known what was going on in his or her institution." This widespread belief exists despite the fact that Blau (1970, 1972), in classic studies of the bureaucratic structure, found two interesting aspects of bureaucracies. The first is that communication within bureaucracies becomes less, not more, reliable as the information

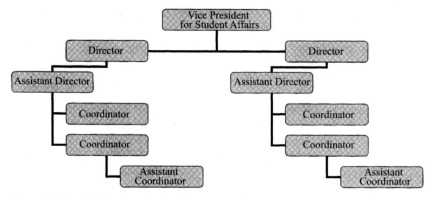

Figure 4.1 Pyramid Style Organizational Structure

progresses up the hierarchy. Blau attributes this phenomenon to the fact that few are willing to report their mistakes to superiors. So, as the communication goes up the hierarchy, the negative aspects of the situation are weakened, leaving the report an unrealistically positive version of the original account. Second, despite the common folklore about "large bureaucracies" and the control inherent in them, Blau found that larger bureaucracies are more diffuse and less apt to be controlled centrally than smaller bureaucracies. This tendency is attributed to the fact that the leader (i.e., person at the top) cannot possibly comprehend all the activity, communication, and knowledge that abounds in a large organization. Instead, trusted staff are relied upon to know and do their jobs with minimal supervision and oversight. The corporate scandals of the 1990s and early 21st century (e.g., Enron, Worldcom) provide evidence that this assumption about control in bureaucracies is unwarranted. Such beliefs can place organizational viability and leadership success in jeopardy.

As stated above, the two models of student affairs practice that rely on administrative and organizational theory as the main perspective are Functional Silos and Student Services. These models are discussed below.

Functional Silos Model

The first use of the term "functional silos" in the student affairs literature is difficult to identify. But, arguably, the 1996 *Student Learning Imperative* (ACPA) may have been the first document where the term gained particular currency. The authors of that document used the term "functional silos" in the following context: "As with other units in a college or university, fragmented units that operate as 'functional silos': that is, meaningful collaboration with other units is a [*sic*] serendipitous" (p. 4 of 6). For anyone living in a state or area where farms are prevalent, silos are familiar icons. You can see silos from miles away: they stand like sentinels over the landscape. As devices that store grain or silage, they are an ingenious way to increase the productivity of the farm. But what is readily apparent when you look at silos is that they are not connected. They stand completely on their own, unattached from other structures (and, therefore, other functions of the farm).

They serve their one function, perhaps very well, but that one function is the extent of their usefulness.

In the 1990s, student affairs, after 50 or so years of existence as a field of education, heartily embraced the bureaucratic trend of increased specialization. Despite periodic budget cuts and staff retrenchment, the overall number of student affairs positions on college campuses grew and became more focused. The commonly used word, silos, represented a metaphor to depict disconnection and isolation from other campus offices. While some welcomed this isolation (see vignette below) as a superior way to conduct business, others saw it as an impediment to excellent student affairs practice.

The functional silos model entails the following characteristics: (1) allegiance to the specific functional area literature in lieu of the broad-spectrum student affairs literature; (2) autonomy by function and often by space and resources; (3) decentralization of supervision, professional development, and, oftentimes, goals; (4) in the worst-case scenario, competition among departments for resources and student attention; (5) philosophical assumption that students require different programs, services, and environments that are best offered by distinct and separate offices; and (6) organizational assumption that services, programs, and policies can be well or adequately delivered without or with minimal division-level coordination. Several of these characteristics are illustrated in the following vignette.

The director of residence life at a midsized public institution came into a student affairs division comprised of approximately eight other offices. His unit, residence life, was the largest auxiliary service of the division. In fact, as an auxiliary service, residence life was vastly different from the other functions within the division. Because of the budgetary and programmatic differences between his area and the other offices, the director of residence life often felt out of place at the division staff meetings. While there were some overlapping goals concerning student development, interventions exercised with the students, and coordination with discipline issues, the director still felt that his area entailed management and administrative issues that were profoundly different—particularly of a different magnitude—than the other division functions. At a staff meeting, the director of residence life expressed his frustration at this situation by saying, "Sometimes I feel that I don't have to interact at all with the rest of you. My department is so different that it really stands on its own in terms of unique financial obligations to the institution, staff issues, and the need to serve students as customers." The director liked the autonomy of determining his own budget and independent personnel decisions and was frustrated by the divisional attempts to coordinate efforts across the various offices.

As this vignette indicates, there are power and resource implications to the functional silos model. A department can afford to be independent if resources are available to support that independence. If one needs to share or borrow resources to be effective, such independence and autonomy is ill advised. Even with independent resources, one wonders at the utility of failing to form a professional community with the other staff. In fact, the DEEP research found that the formation of silos adversely effected student engagement and success.

DEEP Themes and the Functional Silos Model

One of the remarkable aspects of the 20 DEEP project schools was that the functional silos model was minimal. Walls of specialization did not separate the various offices. Instead, there was seamlessness among the services, programs, and functions at these institutions. This was certainly the case within student affairs divisions, but the seamlessness also extended to the academic/student affairs connections.

> The collaborative spirit and positive attitude that characterize DEEP campuses are evident in the quality of working relationships enjoyed by academic and student affairs which operate on many other campuses as functional silos, a situation which is all too common in higher education. (Kuh et al., 2005, p. 172)

This "blurring" effect mimics the approach students take to services, programs, and functions. Rarely do students make distinctions between academic and student life, tenured faculty members and graduate assistants, offices in one division as opposed to another. Instead, to students, college life is one big seamless whole where classes are taken, help obtained, and programs attended by a variety of offices identified as part of the university or college, not a specific part of that institution. At the DEEP project institutions, collaboration is the means to the seamlessness that students experience. Administrators and faculty must know their colleagues, institutional tasks, and the relationship between institutional mission and the function being performed to enact the seamlessness felt by the students.

> Almost all staff and faculty [at George Mason University] we spoke with mentioned that a supportive environment was created based on the collaboration of various units on campus. Few work in silos. The Office of Academic Student Affairs is an example of this type of collaboration, which combines the functions of these two areas that are usually distinct on campuses. . . . The Academic Advising Center is based on collaboration with department faculty, the Career Center, Orientation, and a variety of other offices. There is also a notion of a seamless handoff with academic advising. (NSSE, 2003b, p. 38)

Collaboration dismantles silos or does not allow them to emerge in the first place. An administrator at the University of Kansas commented, "If students are going to have good access to services, then the people who run those services have to have access to each other" (NSSE, 2003d, pp. 41–42).

Strengths of the Functional Silos Model

The first, and most significant, strength of the functional silos model is the staff member expertise available to students. These professionals know their fields extremely well and often undertake the most cutting-edge practice within their area. They are specialists with strong pro-fessional links to student affairs educators outside the institution who occupy similar silos. Because of this emphasis on expertise, students receive a high level of service and program delivery. This expertise also translates into high levels of professionalism.

Another strength that can quickly become a weakness is the presence of independent, stand-alone budgets often called "responsibility-centered budgeting." The expression "every tub on its own bottom" describes this approach. This currently popular budget model is extremely well suited to the functional silos model. Every office, whether an auxiliary service or a general fund-based office, is respon-sible for its income and expenses. For the model to work, autonomy accompanied with professional expertise must be granted to the individual office.

A third strength of the functional silos model is the administrative and organizational clarity afforded by this model. Because of the adherence to the specialization tendency of bureaucracies, the division of labor and specialization of task is clear. This clarity, though, is more obvious to administrators than students because the former are familiar with the organizational principles upon which functional silos are built. Students, on the other hand, are not only unfamiliar with the bureaucratic assumptions, they may use a completely different organizational logic (e.g., functions grouped as they are chronologically experienced in college, by related functions, or by location in the same building) than the logic employed by administrators. Students, therefore, become confused and perhaps frustrated when negotiating the system.

Weaknesses of the Functional Silos Model

In addition to the strengths of the model, the functional silos model contains several weaknesses. The most significant one is that the model is administration centered rather than student centered. Since student affairs is basically and ultimately about serving students, this administrative-centered approach begs the question, who are we ultimately there to serve?

A second weakness of the functional silos model is the professional isolation that may result from the distinctive specialization of the offices. This isolation can quickly turn into professional solitude and lack of community. With these elements, the potential for staff burnout increases. Some of this isolation and burnout may emanate from the homogeneity of theoretical perspective and approach. Any monocultural, singular approach is likely to be weaker than heterogeneous approaches where diversity of experience, approach, and theoretical perspective are emphasized.

A third weakness of the functional silos model is that the existence of stand-alone, independent units means that these offices can be eliminated more easily during budget cuts or shifts in approach. Because the offices are isolated and only loosely coupled to other campus offices, such changes can result in a quick eradication of the whole unit.

Finally, such monotheoretical emphasis as is present in the functional silos model can lead staff to exaggerate their self-importance (see residence life director vignette above). This situation can cause student affairs staff to lose perspective about the centrality of their area to the overall mission of student and academic affairs.

> *A private institution of 5,000 students, nonreligiously affiliated, has a long history of strictly separate academic and student affairs units. Described as the "other side of the house," both sets of personnel are comfortable with the dichotomy that has evolved. While the student affairs units have adopted a learning approach over the past 15 years, spurred by association publications such as the* Student Learning Imperative *(ACPA, 1996) and* Learning Reconsidered *(ACPA & NASPA, 2004), they function as a separate silo from the academic learning perspective. Occasionally, conflict arises within the institution over where offices that exist on the boundary between academic and student affairs (e.g., academic advising, career development) belong within the organization. Some argue that these offices clearly lie within the academic realm. Others argue that the offices are a student affairs function. Because this conflict is rarely resolved on a philosophical or administrative basis, offices switch back and forth between the provost and student affairs divisions. The decisions about where to locate these offices are often made on the strength or weakness of personalities (e.g., vice president, staff members).*

A second administrative-centered student affairs model is the student services model.

Student Services Model

In the student services model, functions and services often are clustered together: financial aid, registrar, and admissions; orientation, academic advising, and admissions; academic advising, counseling, and students with disabilities services. These services and offices generally are not organized under student affairs but are, instead, associated with financial services, student accounts, and the bursar's offices. Although traditional student affairs functions such as student activities and residential life may take a student services approach, in this chapter, the classic student services offices are discussed.

Several assumptions underlie the student services model including beliefs about the purpose of student affairs, expectations about the standard of service, and necessity (or lack thereof) of a student development approach. The first assumption of the student services model is that the main purpose of student affairs is to deliver services, not provide a developmentally oriented education to students. In other words, proponents of the student services model do not assume that all administrators, staff, and faculty are involved in the development of students. From this assumption flows the belief that student services and the developmental/educational aspects of student affairs can be separate. As with any administrative-based organization, some functions provide services and convenience that support the goals of education, not a provision of the education itself. It is not that student development is not a goal of the campus. Rather, a developmental approach to the provision of services is not assumed.

A second assumption of the student services model is that students deserve and are more satisfied when services are conveniently organized and provided. The convenience and high standard of quality is to be provided in part because students pay tuition for those services but, more important, because they are members of the campus community. This assumption is built on a perspective that suggests that students

> prefer a relationship (with the institution) like those they already enjoy with their bank, the telephone company, and the supermarket. . . . They want their colleges nearby and operating at the hours most useful to them, preferably around the clock. They want convenience: easy, accessible parking (in the classroom would not be at all bad); no lines; and polite, helpful and efficient staff service. (Levine & Cureton, 1998, p. 50)

Characteristics of the Student Services Model

The first characteristic of the student services model is that students access the services organized under this model on a periodic, rather than daily, basis. Students consume these services as the need arises. Second, institutions often use enrollment management, total quality management, and other customer-oriented management approaches from the corporate sector to promote a "one-stop-shopping" approach for the convenience of students. This consumer approach, often short term, usually precludes a developmental or student learning perspective. Third, the maintenance of efficient bureaucratic procedures, often a priority, is not always achieved. This is the case because the student services model is built on a use and service provision business-oriented model. Fourth, in the student service model, individual relationships between students and administrators are not as crucial as the overall reputation of the office. Staff in student affairs offices built on a developmental model expect to build personal relationships with students. Student services offices, on the other hand, expect to remain in the public rather than private sphere of students' lives.

Unlike the functional silos model, which can be applied to any area of student affairs practice, the student services model does not fit certain areas of student affairs practice. One might be hard pressed to use this model in student activities, disciplinary affairs, and service learning. Several traditional areas within student affairs (e.g., residence life, career services), while usually adopting a developmental approach, could utilize the student services model and perspective. Some areas (e.g., financial aid, admissions) are more congruent with this approach.

John Jones, a student at Green Mountain University [a pseudonym], has student loans to cover the costs of college. Each semester, he visits the financial aid office to sign forms, process his loans, and apply the loan money to his bill. His family situation is complicated because his parents are divorced and pay for college separately. The family communication often is incomplete so he depends on the financial aid staff to help him understand the outstanding balance on his university bill and other aspects of his finances. Although he visits the office each semester, he has not formed a relationship with any one staff member. He feels comfortable with any of the staff available and is impressed with their level of professionalism and care. Their systems are organized in such a way that, even if he is talking with a staff member he has never interacted with before, the staff member is quickly apprised of his situation. Any staff member he has talked to about financial aid reflects the same experience. The staff know their jobs and are able to help a wide variety of students who walk through the door. He has never had to wait for a particular staff member who is more familiar with his situation than another.

Strengths of the Student Services Model

The student services model contains several inherent strengths. The first is convenience for students. In fact, the model is premised on convenience. In the 1980s, this approach was highlighted in student affairs through the use of total quality management (TQM) as a way to promote excellence in service to the customer. Although many in student affairs took issue with the word "customer," the idea of maintaining a high quality of service is certainly a worthy goal.

A second strength of the student services model is that it creates the space for those who work on teaching, the primary mission of the institution, to be unimpeded by service demands. Faculty and student affairs educators both can get on with the business of education when students' tuition is collected, loans are processes, and registration completed. Related to this strength is the idea that the student services model and the functions entailed with this approach support the infrastructure of the institution: resources are generated, courses are filled, and students are admitted.

A third strength of the student services model is that these services are more readily coordinated with the goals and purposes of institution-wide initiatives such as enrollment management. The coordination necessary between offices that support the infrastructure of the institution creates an opportunity to trace student progress, track student achievement, and understand student attrition. Although traditional development approaches to student affairs play an important role in enrollment management, their more general educational goals and outcomes lack the precision of the student services approach.

Weaknesses of the Student Services Model

The primary weakness of the student services model is obvious: lack of integration of various functions and services. When functions are delineated into specialized areas, the model does not provide an administrative or organizational structure for integration. Without integration, offices are disconnected, miscommunication is common, and institutional goals are only partially met. In other words, services that students may think should logically be grouped together are, instead, separated into offices with little or no overlap. Various attempts (e.g., clustering offices by similar functional areas) to integrate student services functions have been attempted. An innovative model at Trenton State College (now the College of New Jersey) in the 1980s clustered student affairs functions by "individual" student services (e.g., counseling, health services, career services) and group student services (e.g., residence life, student activities, student center). This, like others, was an attempt to bring together student affairs staff with similar functions to better integrate their functions and more skillfully serve students.

A second weakness of the student services model and one related to the lack of integration is the lost opportunity for collaboration between academic and student affairs professionals. In recent years, student affairs practice has increased in complexity and pace. The demands of our work increased to its current fever pitch. As the pace and complexity increased, opportunities for collaboration decreased. Collaboration has many benefits in the long run: better communication, greater creativity, improved staff relations, enriched learning experiences, and enhanced service to students. In the short run, however, collaboration is viewed as time consuming and unnecessary. When services and programs are separate, the opportunities for natural collaboration between and among offices are strained. Attempts to build collaboration to increase collegiality and familiarity with the services available can be artificial in the student services model. Innovative cross-office programs that serve students and professional development programs become "in addition to" the basic work performed by the individual unit. These lost opportunities for collaboration have a more long-lasting effect than immediately realized. The more innovative approaches of new science and quantum theory, when applied to leadership and management, identify collaboration as an essential step to high-quality management in the 21st century (Allen & Cherrey, 2000; Wheatley, 1994; Zohar, 1997). In organizations as complex as colleges and universities, leaders must have the ability to view the whole. Allen and Cherrey talk about "getting on the balcony" to achieve this wholeness perspective. This connection and attention to the whole was emphasized most notably at Alverno College, a DEEP project institution.

> Alverno non-teaching staff members also passionately endorse the emphasis on the whole. For example, the Student Services division

promotes itself as "Partners in Learning in developing a community of learners." In fact, the Partners in Learning strategy resulted from efforts within the division to identify the ways in which Alverno's mission, curriculum, and students shaped their work. According to one staff member, "We see ourselves as an extension of the classroom. We're all important to student learning and we constantly build on the curriculum." For example, student services staff "help students translate their learning into different settings and call them to reflect on their experiences" outside the classroom as well as in. (NSSE, 2003a, p. 12)

If one uses an emphasis on discrete and separate student services offices, wholeness and collaboration are elusive concepts. This deemphasis on collaborative and holistic approaches to management will not serve students and student affairs as a field well in the future.

DEEP Themes and the Administrative-Centered Models
A quality of the student services model that emerged from the DEEP study was the use of student employees as essential members of the college staff. University of Maine Farmington was easily the exemplar of this approach.

Student services . . . employs students. . . . They have close contact with faculty, staff and supervisors, and obtain significant responsibilities over the course of their college career. Funding for student clubs is largely coordinated and monitored by student employees. The wellness program (aerobics classes, etc.) at the student fitness center also is coordinated and—for the most part—taught by students. Students also serve on a number of University committees. One example is particularly striking: We heard from a young man who was asked by an administrator to spearhead the construction of a new Education facility according to "green" standards. The student has taken it upon himself to become an advocate for the project by educating himself about the green movement and the realities of the project budget. "I thought I was going to have to push a boulder up a hill. Instead, it's been positive. I felt like a professional. I had to know my stuff. The President is pretty serious. She made sure I knew my stuff," he explained. It was on the basis of this student's initiative—involving significant research which he then had to present before faculty and administrators—that the University made a commitment to "green" buildings in planning for new construction. (NSSE, 2003e, pp. 28–29)

In addition to Farmington, Gonzaga University in Spokane, Washington, amply uses student staff as a way to teach leadership as well as provide staff support in an institutional climate of scare resources.

Student life and student services offices not only hire students to augment full-time staff, these students are essential to ensuring the delivery of quality services to peers. Often, student staff members' responsibilities are on par with entry-level full-time staff. (NSSE, 2003c, p. 31)

A final aspect related to administrative affinity models and the DEEP research is the relationship to the physical environment. If student services are to be efficiently and effectively delivered to students, their physical placement must be considered. Student affairs has long considered the effect of the environment on student learning. The early campus ecology movement (Banning, 1978) and the more recent campus environments literature (Strange & Banning, 2001) eloquently speak to the importance of matching physical considerations to learning and developmental goals.

Align the physical environment with institutional priorities and goals for student success. Rather than putting student services on the perimeter of the campus, or in out of the way places, student services at DEEP institutions were centrally located and easy to find (Kuh et al., 2005, p. 314).

Summary

The lack of a holistic perspective and absent collaborative approach of the functional silos and student services models encourage competitive rather than collaborative approaches to student affairs. The two administrative-centered models discussed in this chapter and critiqued in *The Student Learning Imperative* (ACPA, 1996) emphasize a nonintegrated, decentralized approach that does not serve students or the learning goals of the campus as well as other choices. When only the VPSA has a bird's eye view on the division, directors may be apt to adopt a decentralized approach where competition rather than cooperation is the standard operating procedure. Students cannot help but be served inadequately when competition as opposed to cooperation and decentralization as opposed to integration are the norms. Unhealthy competition may occur about funding acquired, number of students served, and staff positions obtained. At its worst, competition breeds empire building and myopia. Directors argue for their individual offices rather than maintaining a view that takes the good of the entire division and institution into account. With an emphasis on decentralization and discrete operations, unit directors may feel that they need not interact with other directors within their division.

Since the mid-1990s, the emphasis in student affairs has been less on administrative-centered models and more on learning-centered approaches. While the administrative-centered approach is not as current as in the formative days of the student affairs field, these models, depending on institutional mission, retain their currency. These models have the most saliency in

- Institutions with first-generation college students or others who need clear pathways for success (Kuh et al., 2005);
- Students with multiple demands such as family and full-time positions;
- Institutions (e.g., Ivy Leagues, specialized institutions) without a traditional student affairs mission;
- Institutions with complex processes for graduation, course requirements, and other administratively complicated procedures.

As student affairs administrators, particularly senior student affairs officers, make decisions about the ways to organize a division of student affairs, the strengths and weaknesses of the models discussed in this chapter can be considered. Perhaps it is possible to take the strengths of these models (e.g., quality of service to students, expertise present in staff) and weave those into models that more adequately reflect the current learning-centered approaches to student affairs practice.

CHAPTER 5

LEARNING-CENTERED MODELS

One of the foundational elements of contemporary student affairs practice is student learning. While learning has been an emphasis of student affairs practice, directly or indirectly, at least since the publication of *The Student Personnel Point of View, 1937* (ACE), the release of *The Student Learning Imperative* (ACPA, 1996) stimulated consideration and implementation of strategies that were designed to enhance the learning dimension of the student experience. Student affairs practice has been conceptualized to encourage and stimulate student learning (see, for example, Kuh, 1999; Magolda, 1999), and measuring student learning has become an important dimension of student affairs practice (Kuh et al., 2005; Schuh & Upcraft, 2001). Following is an example of how student learning can be operationalized from a seamless learning perspective.

An Example of Seamless Student Experiences

Sean and Marty are sophomores at Eastern University. It is the middle of the academic year. Both are still deciding their majors. Last semester they enrolled in a six-credit course that focused on regional environmental problems, team-taught by a faculty member from the biology department and a faculty member from the political science department. The class met for three hours each Monday and Wednesday morning. The faculty members had an optional brown-bag lunch for the students right after each class session. Most students usually attended the lunch session and the conversation often continued the discussion of the day's class work.

Sean and Marty were members of a learning community of 12 students. They lived on the same floor of their residence hall. The learning group got together each Sunday evening, usually for three or four hours to prepare for class. They also had ad hoc study sessions before exams. One of the course requirements was that students were obligated to present a short research paper to the class, so the members of the team practiced with each other so that their presentations were polished.

Sean had a 10-hour-per-week undergraduate research assistantship with one of the professors. In the assistantship Sean helped two upper-class research assistants do preliminary work on a paper the professor and students planned to present to a regional conference on water policy. If their proposal is accepted, Sean and the other students will travel to the conference late in the spring.

Marty worked with a local public interest group on an internship basis on a project designed to help members of the community conserve water. One of the faculty members from the course helped Marty secure the paid internship. Marty provided a report to the professor at the end of term. A multiyear drought had affected the ground water table in the region where Eastern University is located, and conservation was one strategy that the regional water district recommended. Marty went to local elementary schools and taught water conservation to the students. Marty applied several of the concepts of the course during this internship.

In addition to the work in class each week, the professors and students explored the possibility of forming an environmental club on campus. The appropriate forms were filed with the student activities office and an application for funding was filed with the student senate. The senate will act on the request early in the spring term.

   When the semester was over, the two faculty members had an end-of-semester celebration with the students at one of their homes. The provost's office provides modest funding for faculty to host these kinds of events, and the faculty and students from the course got together one last time to celebrate the end of the semester and talk about what they were planning to do next term.

This example is a collage of experiences of students who attended DEEP project schools. Among the elements of the example are the following experiences that were common to many DEEP institutions:

1. Interdisciplinary courses, team taught by faculty members;
2. Faculty interacting with students outside of class, focusing on coursework;
3. Learning communities;
4. Undergraduate research assistantships;
5. Internships and service learning;
6. Academic clubs; and
7. Faculty and students having social interaction.

This approach to the student experience suggests that student and academic affairs approach the student experience from a similar philosophical perspective and share complementary goals for students at Eastern University. Other approaches to student learning have been taken over time, and while the goal of students having as robust a learning experience as possible is similar, the approach taken can be very different. Several of these traditional models of student affairs practice are discussed below; including the competitive, adversarial model; co-curricular model; and seamless learning model.

The Competitive, Adversarial Model

This type of learning-centered model, in effect, pits student affairs–related activities and experiences against classroom activities. It suggests that academic and student affairs units are concerned with what students learn and how they grow and develop, but it also suggests that neither side is quite willing to reach out to the other to create coordinated, complementary learning experiences for students. While one would hope that this model is not common practice on contemporary college campuses, it is important to recognize that absent a willingness on the part of both units to work together, relationships could evolve to a circumstance reflected by this model.

The competitive dimension of this model may reflect unintended, yet real, competition for students' attention and time. Experiences, opportunities, and activities are planned without regard to what the other unit is doing. This may result in duplication of effort in some cases, while in others students may be forced to choose between equally worthy opportunities. The adversarial dimension of this model may take hold in an example like this:

> A course coordinator for an entry-level science course schedules the midterm examination at the beginning of the semester. At the same time, and without consulting the course schedule, the student activities office, in conjunction with an upper-class student service organization, schedules the annual weekend dance marathon to raise funds for a local charity. Typically this is an all-campus event that has a high level of participation on the part of many students. The marathon dimension of the activity is that it runs continuously from Friday night through Sunday morning, and students raise money through 36 hours of continuous activities. By the time it is over, the students are exhausted, and need the balance of the weekend to catch up on their sleep. Very little studying occurs over this weekend. In the end, many students are not as well prepared (or rested) for the important midterm science exam. The course coordinator is frustrated because students do not do as well as they should have on the exam, and as a consequence, lets the academic dean know. The academic dean complains to the dean of students about the situation, and, in turn, the student activities staff are notified. They are unhappy because the fundraiser is scheduled the same weekend every year and it is widely publicized. Can't the faculty member pay attention to the institutional calendar of events?

History of the Competitive, Adversarial Model
Specialization and narrowness of focus increasingly have been features of higher education and it is no wonder that the various units found in a

division of student affairs often have mimicked this pattern. Although student affairs functions began informally, perhaps when avuncular faculty members provided advice to homesick students, the appointment of the first dean, at Harvard University in 1870 (Nuss, 2003), marks the formal beginning of student affairs work. As the formal academic dimension has become more specialized over the years, so too has student affairs. Even though some academic departments began in the second half of the 1700s (Hecht, Higgerson, Gmelch, & Tucker, 1999), it was much later that this organizational structure was common. Although student affairs practice became specialized later than what occurred in the formal, academic dimensions of higher education, it followed a similar model of specialization over time. Over the years such areas of practice as placement, counseling services, residence hall programs, student activities, and others emerged. And, as faculty chose to divest themselves of certain academic support functions, such areas as academic advising and the registrar's functions became part of the student affairs portfolio.

Along with increasing specialization in higher education came growth. The history of institutions of higher education, particularly state universities, is that institutions have become larger and more specialized over the years, violating the recommendation of Astin (1977, as cited in Kuh et al., 2005) that undergraduate enrollments should not be greater than 15,000. For example, in fall 1996, 350 institutions had an enrollment of 10,000 or more (The *Chronicle* 1999–2000 Almanac) but by fall 2001, the number of institutions with an enrollment of more than 10,000 was 451 (The *Chronicle* Almanac 2004–5). This means that an additional 101 institutions approached a level of enrollment that would make them less desirable using Astin's perspective, in just five years. And, within this growth, 14 more institutions had an enrollment of over 30,000 in 2001 than was the case in 1996. Why? To accommodate an increasingly larger percentage of the population that seeks postsecondary education, it is easier and cheaper to accommodate enrollments through enrollment growth than through building new campuses.

One consequence of increasingly large undergraduate enrollments is that communication between the various elements of a university (e.g., academic departments and student affairs units) becomes increasingly difficult as institutions grow. Similarly, communication between individuals becomes more difficult because as institutions grow in size, individuals simply will know an increasingly smaller percentage of the faculty and staff as institutions get larger.

One cannot expect institutions to get smaller, particularly in the face of increasingly larger percentages of high school graduates attending college. The National Center for Education Statistics (2005) reported increasing participation rates in postsecondary education over a 30-year period from 1974 through 2003 and projects a rate of increase that will continue to accelerate through 2013 (National Center for Education Statistics, 2004). So, in the face of growing enrollments, the tendency is for individuals to increasingly specialize. This growth leads to "compartmentalization and fragmentation, often resulting in what is popularly described as '*functional silos*' [italics added] or '*mine shafts*' [itailics added]" (Schroeder, 1999a, p. 137, emphasis added). Insularity, according to Schroeder, is the likely result of these developments.

Philosophy of the Competitive, Adversarial Model

Young (1996) wrote of the philosophical tensions between the student personnel point of view and a philosophy of practice. In the case of the example of the weekend dance marathon, the philosophy of practice focuses on service and conceptualizes the student experience as individualistic and segregated. A consequence of this approach is that student affairs practitioners work hard at providing the very best experiences and services possible for students, within the framework of their departments. The coordinator of student activities tries to develop the best leadership development program possible, without really thinking about how the program could be linked to leadership development in the College of Business. Or, the volunteer coordinator develops an outstanding program for students at the local youth shelter, but does not realize that the sociology department may be trying to do the same thing with service learning.

This does not mean that administrative actions are guided by lack of interest in working together, or an unwillingness to cooperate. Rather, individuals strive to do the best they can within their sphere of influence, and since few others reach out to develop collaborative relationships, the culture evolves to the point where specialization rules the day. Once in motion, this model results in increasing specialization, attention to improvement within the silo, and focus on doing one's narrow definition of "work better." The consequence of this approach is that opportunities are frequently missed.

Features of the Competitive, Adversarial Model

The features of the competitive, adversarial model illustrate the lack of communication and collaboration of the academic and student affairs staff.

Distinctive Missions. The missions of academic affairs and student affairs are crafted in this model as if neither unit were aware of the contributions that the units can make to each other. Student affairs staff members conceptualize their contributions to student learning as occurring outside the classroom or laboratory and they think primarily about the psychosocial development of students. The cognitive development of students is left to the faculty and classrooms. Important in the student affairs approach to student life is providing distinctive learning experiences for students, that may or may not complement other experiences of students on campus. That is, what students learn from their out-of-class experiences is a consequence of a specific experience as opposed to a series of experiences linked to other experiences on campus. Leadership development, for example, may be provided in the residence halls, student activities, Greek affairs, or through academic departments such as communications or the honors program. In the case of this illustration, four units could be engaged in leadership development independently of one another.

Independence of Work. As the leadership training example suggests, the work of the various units on campus is conducted separate of one another. This leads to overlapping and duplicative efforts. The approach tends to be quite inefficient because more than one unit may be devoting resources to similar student experience when they could work together to provide a more robust, less costly set of experiences for students.

Locus of Learning. The location where student experience occurs is important. That is, certain forms of learning are conceptualized in certain places. For example, psychosocial development is thought of as resulting from out-of-class experiences. Cognitive development is left to formal, academic experiences, usually within a classroom, laboratory, or library. Rather than thinking that various types of student learning could occur virtually anywhere at any time, this conceptual approach is that certain kinds of learning can only occur in certain places. So, some forms of learning are reserved for the formal curriculum, and other forms of learning are the territory of the out-of-class experience. An example of this could be that the residence life staff decides to organize a tutoring program for students who are enrolled in the math course that most first-year students take. At the same time the supplemental instruction program offers a program for first-year students who are taking the entry-level math course. Neither office thinks to contact the other to determine if they could collaborate on such a program. As such, the staff work in their own silos.

Organizational Boundaries. Student life is conceptualized as occurring in segments, and staff from student affairs do not think to work with academic affairs staff on common issues. Similarly, academic affairs staff see what occurs outside the classroom as not much more than being social in nature. So, staff from each division of the institution works independently of one another. The consequence can be something like this example:

> *Academic orientation is planned independently of orientation to the residence halls. Receptions for students to meet faculty members in their major areas of study are planned in the late afternoon at the same time a residence hall volleyball tournament is scheduled. Communication about avoiding scheduling conflicts is not even considered, and student participation in both experiences is diluted.*

The Co-Curricular Model

The co-curricular model approach to student affairs acknowledges the growth and development that comes from out-of-class experiences of students, but it also charts an approach that is independent from the learning experiences that result from the formal academic curriculum. An example of this approach to student affairs work is as follows:

> *The senior student affairs staff at Eastern University had a retreat in late summer in preparation for the academic year. Staff were committed to providing learning experiences for students and the purpose of the retreat was to identify a series of opportunities for students for the upcoming year built around two or three themes. This work resulted in the following themes for the year: learning based on leadership development, experiences with diversity, and service to the community. Each of the unit heads in the division agreed to develop a series of programs and other experiences for students built on these themes. Examples of these experiences included a leadership training program for organization officers, a mentor program sponsored by the office of diversity programming, and a series of community service activities for residence hall students. Everyone agreed that these plans would contribute substantially to student growth in their out-of-class experiences for the upcoming year.*
>
> *At the same time the senior academic affairs leaders had a retreat looking at areas of emphasis in faculty development for the upcoming year. They decided that the faculty development program for the year should emphasize pedagogical techniques that feature active learning and applications of classroom learning in practical settings. These leaders agreed that they would work with their department chairs and faculty so as to enhance these dimensions of the formal curriculum during the upcoming academic year and perhaps beyond.*

History of the Co-Curricular Model

The co-curricular model reflects the maturation of the previous model in that it reflects a perspective that a student's college experience is neatly apportioned into elements associated with the formal, credit-bearing curriculum that leads to majors, minors, concentrations and degrees, and into out-of-class experiences leading to psychosocial development. An example of this approach comes from Mueller (1961) who indicated that the student experience consisted of intellectual development and personal development. She asserted that "the intellectual progress of the student should be the concern of everyone, and so should his [*sic*] personal development" (p. 55). Following this line of thinking, then, there are two dimensions of the student experience (intellectual and social development), but according to Mueller those assigned to one dimension or the other should be concerned about both.

Although it is difficult to identify a precise time when this philosophy was prevalent, since undoubtedly there are institutions today where this approach frames student affairs work, one marker of this approach can be found in the observation of Brown (1972) who wrote, "In the past the threads of intellectual and student development ran parallel, but in more recent years the theorists have suggested that they should be intertwined" (p. 29).

Philosophy of the Co-Curricular Model

The guiding philosophy of this student learning model is that institutions of higher education are responsible for the growth of the student, but faculty and others who deliver the academic program are responsible for students' intellectual development and student affairs staff address the social and out-of-class experiences and development of students. Partnering across organizational lines is not common in this approach. The academic and student affairs staff cede responsibility to each other and tend to stay out of each other's way. Each side respects the professionalism of the other and tries not to interfere with the other's work. This approach might be thought of as functional silos in the most positive sense of the term. That is, the work of the various units is done by well-prepared, highly informed people who strive to stay focused on their work and not interfere with that of others on campus.

Features of the Co-Curricular Model

The model has features that are similar to the competitive, adversarial model, but they are operationalized far differently.

Complementary, but Separate Missions. In this model the missions of academic and student affairs are distinct, but the units acknowledge the contributions of each other to the student experience. Student affairs is concerned with the out-of-class development of students and academic affairs focuses on what students learn in their classroom experiences. What students learn outside of the formal curriculum is perceived to be important, but secondary, to what is learned inside the curriculum.

Independent Work. Student affairs and academic affairs work independently of one another, but members of the various units do communicate with one another on important issues. For example, a joint orientation committee plans the events and experiences for new students each fall. Members of the committee recognize that both academic and student affairs contribute to the orientation process, and time is reserved for each unit to offer experiences for students. But, the planning of an orientation schedule is more about avoiding scheduling conflicts and really not about collaborating to plan events that are designed to facilitate student learning from multiple perspectives.

Contributions to Student Learning. Student affairs staff are committed to contributing to student learning, but in their own sphere of influence. Rather than trying to collaborate with faculty or academic affairs staff, the student affairs staff plan their student learning experiences on their own. An example of this is a community service program planned for residence hall students. Several residence hall staff members have solid connections with community leaders in the neighboring town. They begin to work with these leaders on various community service projects. These are successful and the students who participate learn a great deal from them. Residence life staff members do not consider contacting faculty in the sociology department to determine if they would have an interest in weaving such experiences into their courses and perhaps develop a service-learning program. The culture does not work that way.

Locus of Learning Is Distinguished. The mindset related to this model is that certain kinds of learning will occur from specific experiences on campus, and that overlap does not occur. This means that learning related to courses, credits, and ultimately what a baccalaureate degree signifies results from formal, academic experiences, and other learning experiences, potentially significant, result from the co-curriculum. Among these outcomes would be leadership development, understanding the value of interacting with people of cultures different from one's own, and contributing to one's community. The model does not recognize the complementary nature of student experiences.

Boundaries Characterize the Work Environment. In spite of the acknowledgment of the contributions of various parts of the institution to student learning, boundaries demarcate where staff from the various units can deliver learning experiences. Faculty, for example, would not consider offering a residentially based program. They do not feel welcome taking a meal with students in the residence halls, even if they were invited to do so. Student affairs staff would not consider proposing to offer an experience for credit, even though they would be qualified to do so under the institution's faculty personnel policies. The formal curriculum and co-curriculum are defined, and the boundaries between the two are crossed only in rare situations.

Seamless Learning Model

The seamless learning model suggests that the institution has adopted a philosophy that student learning has the potential to result from virtually all student experiences. Structures are in place so that academic and student affairs leaders are aware of developments in each division of the institution, and ideas for working together on issues related to student learning are suggested routinely. Consider this example:

> *At Eastern University senior members of student affairs have been considering various ideas to enrich the quality of residential life. Residence life staff as well as others in the division have believed for a year or so that the quality of residential life was not what it could be. After discussion at the VPSA cabinet meeting, the decision was made to consider initiatives along these lines. The residence life staff, which instigated the discussion, was instructed to develop two to four proposals that would have the potential to improve the quality of the student experience.*
>
> *The organizational structure of the division is such that a senior member of the provost's staff, the associate provost for student learning, regularly attends the division's meetings. Similarly, the assistant vice president for student life attends the provost's staff meetings. In developing these quality-of-residential-life-enhancement proposals, the residence life staff asks the associate provost to participate in the discussions and the development of the proposals. Two that emerged were the development of learning*

communities and a plan by which students could invite faculty members to join them for meals in the residence halls at no cost to the faculty member.

A joint meeting of the senior staff in student affairs and academic affairs was called to consider the proposals. After carefully considering the advantages and disadvantages of the proposals, the learning communities proposal was adopted but the meal program was not. From this group the VPSA and the provost appointed the core of an implementation task force that would identify how the details of the learning communities project would be addressed.

History of the Seamless Learning Model

As was reported above, Brown (1972) questioned the co-curricular approach that was in vogue at the time of his writing, but it took a number of years before documents began to emerge that recognized the connectedness of the student experience. Howard Bowen's volume (1977) included the following observation: "Education, or the teaching-learning function, is defined to embrace not only the formal academic curricula, classes and laboratories but also those influences upon students flowing from the many and varied experience of campus life" (p. 33). Bowen identified a number of historical documents related to this concept (i.e., that higher education should be concerned with the whole student experience). The Study Group on the Conditions of Excellence in American Higher Education (1984) emphasized that "perhaps the most important [condition] for improving undergraduate education—is student involvement" (p. 17). The NASPA (1989) in its document *Points of View* asserted, "Out-of-class social and physical environments are rarely neutral; they help or detract from students' social and intellectual development" (p. 13). All of this work and that of others (e.g., Astin, 1993; Kuh et al., 1991; Tinto, 1993) led to the paper *The Student Learning Imperative* (ACPA, 1996), which provided the trigger for the current emphasis on student learning, irrespective of whether this learning occurs in a classroom, in a residence hall, or somewhere else, on or off campus. Subsequent work (e.g., Schuh & Whitt, 1999; Kuh et al., 2005) has provided additional ideas on the extent to which institutions can create partnerships and conditions that facilitate student learning.

Philosophy of the Seamless Learning Model

The Student Learning Imperative indicates that the mission of a student affairs division committed to student learning "complements the institution's mission, with the enhancement of student learning and personal development being the primary goal of student affairs programs and services" (ACPA, 1996, p. 119). The document added another characteristic of the learning-oriented student affairs division: "Student affairs professionals collaborate with other institutional agents and agencies to promote student learning and personal development" (p. 120).

Kuh (1996) built on *The Student Learning Imperative* and advocated that colleges and universities strive to create seamless learning environments. In this case, seamless refers to

> what was once believed to be separate, distinct parts (e.g., in-class and out-of-class, academic and non-academic, curricular and cocurricular, or on-campus and off-campus experiences) are now of one piece, bound together so as to appear whole or continuous. (p. 136)

Thus, instead of working in silos, to provide the best possible experiences for students regardless of what was occurring elsewhere on campus, student affairs professionals and faculty, guided by this philosophy, need to tear down their silos and develop integrated, complementary experiences for students. This philosophy suggests that the whole of the student experience is greater than the sum of its parts, that no persons or units possess sufficient expertise that other units or people cannot add value by working with them, and that the student experience is best conceived of as an ongoing developmental process that begins when a student applies for admission and ends, in a formal sense, at graduation.

Features of the Seamless Learning Model

The features of this model are such that academic and student affairs work together to contribute to the student experience.

Collaborative Missions. In this model, the mission of the institution is dedicated to student learning. The missions of both academic and student affairs are designed to contribute to the total student learning experience. The institution is dedicated to providing a robust, enriched learning experience for students, and academic and student affairs are dedicated to contributing to this total learning experience to which the institution is committed.

Collaborative Efforts. Representatives from academic and student affairs recognize that what students learn is what the institution has dedicated itself to, and they work together to devise ways to enhance learning. An example is the approach to orientation programs. Before planning any programming, the members of the orientation committee work together to identify the learning outcomes they believe are most desirable from orientation for new students. After doing a thorough study related to these outcomes, programs are planned with these outcomes in mind. Some programs are planned primarily by academic affairs while the student affairs staff plans others, but the orientation committee closely monitors the planning of the experiences and a master calendar is kept so that the various experiences can be linked to the learning outcomes desired for students. Recall the example of the volleyball tournament and departmental receptions conflicting during orientation under the competitive model. Using a seamless learning approach, the volleyball matches might be scheduled on an afternoon of orientation week on the lawn adjacent to an academic building where open houses are held simultaneously and the afternoon could conclude with a student-faculty picnic.

Everyone Contributes to Student Learning. In this model the assumption is that every member of the institution can contribute to learning. This means that everyone's ideas are worth considering, and that the value of one's contributions is not linked to one's formal institutional role. The cafeteria staff member may have an idea on how to enrich student-faculty conversations in the dining hall. The grounds crew member might have an idea on how to use the lawns of the institution for picnics or other student-faculty interaction.

In- and Out-of-Classroom Learning Is Blurred. The potential for student learning is recognized no matter what students and faculty are doing. While students are expected to learn in class, it also means that experiences can be developed for them to learn outside of class. As institutional priorities change or evolve, what may have been the territory of the out-of-class experiences of students may be infused into the curriculum or vice versa. The driving force for what students learn is an unwavering commitment to achieving the mission and goals of the institution. Various units dedicate themselves to devising ways that they can work together so that students have the best learning experiences possible.

Boundaries Are Indistinguishable. Whereas in the other models it was easy to identify the boundaries between various units on campus and what students learned in or out of class, boundaries are difficult to identify on campuses that adopt this model. To be sure, students receive formal credit for their academic work, but their academic work might occur in class, outside of class on campus, or in the local community. Members of the various units collaborate to provide the best learning experiences possible, driven by the mission of the institution and the learning experiences desired for students. Academic and student affairs work together on such experiences as service learning, tutoring, leadership development, and internships.

Conclusion

This chapter was designed to discuss three models of student affairs practice that focus on student learning. Although they have the same general goal, that is, trying to identify services, programs, and activities that contribute to student learning, the approaches taken vary dramatically. In one case the division of student affair operates very much independently of the rest of the institution. In another case, student affairs stays focused on the social development of students and is very careful to avoid the other forms of student learning that occur on campus. In the third approach presented, units from the division of student affairs collaborate regularly with academic affairs to provide the best experiences possible for students. Our obvious bias is toward the third model, since, in our judgment, this approach has the potential to provide the most robust experiences for students. Our study of the

20 DEEP institutions leads us to draw this conclusion, since we saw literally hundreds of examples of student affairs and faculty collaboration develop learning experiences for students. We think this approach provides excellent promise for increasing the robustness of the student learning experience on contemporary college campuses.

PART III

INNOVATIVE PROPOSED MODELS BASED ON DEEP RESEARCH

CHAPTER 6

STUDENT-CENTERED
INNOVATIVE MODELS

Students have always been at the center of the student affairs profession. Beginning with *The Student Personnel Point of View, 1937* (ACE, 1937), the profession claimed as its central purpose the education of the whole student. This emphasis intensified as student affairs accepted chief responsibility for responding to the needs of new nontraditional students brought into higher education through the GI Bill. The adoption of the philosophy of student development afforded the profession the authority of being a strong voice for students in the academy. Student development theory has furthered the view that students are at the center of the academy.

Early approaches to student affairs practice such as those described in chapter 3 emphasize student affairs responsibility for student needs in the extracurriculum. This approach makes the needs of students preeminent. However, because these needs are typically separated from curricular activities, the approach has been criticized as having limited utility in promoting student learning. As we studied the educationally effective colleges and universities in the DEEP project, we saw evidence of student-centered approaches in student affairs divisions that enhanced student engagement and success. Some institutions developed intrusive developmental support services to respond to student needs, while others elevated students to important roles in campus governance and employed them as paraprofessionals. At a few institutions students were empowered to lead campus initiatives with limited intervention from administrators. These student-centered models appear to originate in the student affairs profession's history of focusing on the development of the whole person, but this idea is expanded on in ways that promote student success.

In this chapter, we outline three innovative approaches to student affairs that retain the view of students at the center of the enterprise, but do so in novel ways to enhance student success. We first describe the student-centered ethic of care model, then the student-driven model, and conclude with the student agency model. Several vignettes are used to introduce the concepts and add context for understanding the models. We then outline the strengths and weaknesses of each approach and consider the relationship between these student affairs models and student success.

Student-Centered Ethic of Care Model

The first model discussed in this chapter is a student-centered ethic of care. Although each model in this chapter places students at the forefront of student affairs practice, this one centers on care and relationships. Gilligan's (1982) ethic of care and Nel Noddings's (1984) expansion of this concept provide theoretical underpinnings of this model's approach marked by a fundamental response to student needs; services geared toward the goal of facilitating student success;

integrated services, policies, and programs; and practice centered on an ethic of care.

In the late 1990s Adams University [a pseudonym] faced significant challenges related to student retention. First-year student retention rates had dropped for four years in a row, and student survey data indicated overall dissatisfaction with the quality of advising, infrequent use of academic support services such as tutoring, and a perception that the institution did little to help students succeed academically. A task force was assembled and charged with determining a plan for improving the situation for students.

The task force report identified recommendations based in student development theory and influential documents like The Student Learning Imperative *and* Making Quality Count, *and detailed a plan titled "Student Success Initiatives." The crux of the plan was the integration of services to more effectively meet the needs of students, particularly in their first year of college. The vice president of student affairs and the provost were put in charge of realizing the vision of the plan.*

One of the first initiatives realized from the plan was the establishment of the Student Success Center. Although services such as advising and tutoring were previously available to students, they were housed in several offices across different divisions. The creation of the Student Success Center integrated services such as tutoring, academic advising, computer instruction, academic skill development, testing and placement, and career exploration. Broadly, the Center served individual needs of students as they persist toward an undergraduate degree and develop into lifelong learners. Specific initiatives for first-year students, including a first-year peer mentoring program and an interactive computer simulation to help students assess their writing, were developed. Most important, the Center afforded the institution the opportunity to more clearly articulate a shared vision and philosophy for student success.

Although the Student Success Center was intended to provide essential services in one convenient location, student affairs units also recognized that to adequately address student advising and general academic support needs, it was necessary to conduct additional outreach. To this end, the Career Development Center sponsored a variety of outreach programs in the residence halls including "Suite Talk," a program that engaged students in their residence hall suites in conversations about setting educational goals, career advising, developing resumes, and securing internships. The Center also collaborated with dining services to offer an etiquette series to

*help seniors gain experience interviewing over a meal. Center staff set as
their goal to conduct one workshop a month in student space.*

This depiction of the Student Success Center development and
enhancement of student support services represents many characteristics of a student-centered ethic of care model. In this model students'
needs are preeminent. "Caring involves stepping out of one's own
personal frame of reference into the other's. When we care, we consider
the other's point of view, his [*sic*] objective needs, and what he expects
of us" (Noddings, 1984, p. 24). Student affairs educators understand
how time consuming working through one student's issues can be.
Whether developmental in an affirmative sense (e.g., orientation leadership training) or reactive (e.g., disciplinary action), the ethic of care
model places students' needs at the center.

History and Theoretical Perspective of the Ethic of Care Model
In 1982, Carol Gilligan wrote a classic work about women's psychological and moral development. *In a Different Voice* has stood the test
of time as a significant work in human development. Generations of
student affairs educators have used her theories to understand psychological development, which is based on an ethic of care rather than
an ethic of justice. Gilligan's work offered several assumptions that
proved to be groundbreaking. The first was that the previous assumed
"neutral" theories of psychological and moral development were actually gender related. Prior to Gilligan, the prevailing theories of human
development (e.g., Kohlberg, Freud, Perry) were crafted from research
on male subjects but generalized to men and women. Women's development, previously considered at a lower level than male development,
was redefined by Gilligan as different, not deficient. "Implicitly adopting the male life as the norm, they [psychological theorists] have tried
to fashion women out of a masculine cloth" (p. 6–7).

The second assumption posited by Gilligan grew from an extension
of Chodorow's theories about the role of relationship in the lives of
women. "Female identity formation takes place in a context of ongoing
relationship since mothers tend to experience their daughters as more
like, and more continuous with, themselves" (Gilligan, 1982, p. 7).
The theory formed was that women's development occurred in the

context of relationship and connection; men's development occurred in the context of autonomy and separation. Since Gilligan's 1982 work, theory about an ethic of care has been debated, refined, and expanded. But, the impact of this early work cannot be underestimated. Its influence on the student affairs field, a field marked by care and connection, has been significant.

The ethic of care model acknowledges that some students come to college inadequately prepared to perform academically at acceptable levels, or may lack the necessary social skills or capital to succeed in college. The model emphasizes that colleges and universities have a moral and educational obligation to provide the academic and social support students need to succeed. Notably, at the educationally effective colleges in the DEEP project, this is not about lowering academic standards or "coddling." Instead, the institutions provide the resources and skill development opportunities students need to improve their performance and meet achievement standards.

The ethic of care model focuses attention on students most in need of support. For example, most institutions pay far more attention to new first-time first-year students than they do to transfer students. As a result, transfers often do not know enough about the available resources, services, and institutional features. Equally problematic, they have little in common with the academic and social experiences of their first-year peers and cannot easily connect with other transfer students. Thus, they often feel disconnected. However, DEEP colleges and universities with an ethic of care model address this challenge with events that welcome and introduce transfer students to the institution. For example, at one institution, about half of the annual incoming class are transfer students. Separate orientation programs and support services are tailored to their needs. Specially designated sections of the semester-long "Introduction to the University" class review university policies, requirements, procedures, and campus resources. Career Services reaches out to and informs transfer students about internship opportunities and, if they are undeclared, about majors. The campus retention committee, representing student and academic affairs, examines transfer student data to ensure that adequate services are provided.

Student affairs divisions organized on the ethic of care model develop services and programs with the goal of facilitating student success and maximizing student development outcomes. When services are linked and safety nets established, fewer students fall through the cracks. These initiatives are even more effective when student and academic affairs collaborate on these efforts.

Strengths of the Ethic of Care Model

One strength of the ethic of care model is clearly the level of service available to students. In this case, "service" is not the same concept as discussed in chapter 4 in the student services model. While the latter is based on administrative expediency and procedure, the ethic of care model premises service provision on the ability of the student affairs educator to devote time to students in need, assist the student in the most sensitive and compassionate means possible, and create a climate in which every member of the community is valued.

A second strength of the ethic of care model is the environment created by an atmosphere of care. When professionals earn a reputation for caring, trust seeps through the college environment. Community building proceeds in an easier manner as students obtain the emotional support necessary to form healthy relationships, engage in constructive risk taking, and pursue developmental tasks that lead to engagement and involvement.

Weaknesses of the Ethic of Care Model

The major weakness of the ethic of care model is glaringly obvious: it is highly time consuming. With budget constraints, increased psychological and emotional needs of students, and the sheer volume of student affairs work growing each year, the labor intensive nature of the ethic of care model may not be possible on many campuses. Another weakness of the ethic of care model is a possibility of treating students in a childlike manner. With a model framed nearly exclusively by care, one must be careful to avoid parental and overly protective approaches to student affairs work. The prevalent models of care often are fashioned on conceptions of proper parenting. Obviously, student affairs educators are not parents but have a long history of *in loco parentis* and paternalism. Any professional using this model must be vigilant so that care does not turn into the coddling discussed above for the student.

Student-Driven Model

The second student-centered model discussed is the student-driven model. Assumptions of this model include trust in students' ability to manage college functions, understanding of the potential of the college environment to teach student leadership, and belief in empowered students.

At Superior University (SU) [a pseudonym], about half of the 3,000 enrolled students live on or within walking distance of campus and almost all are working more than 20 hours a week while enrolled full time. Most entered the university directly out of a high school in the region, and very few are of nontraditional age. Many of the students at SU qualify for Federal Work–Study and most are paying their own way through college. These students work on average up to 30 hours a week to afford education and living expenses. Few are working just to earn spending money or to contribute to insurance payments on late model cars. However, despite the fact that SU students are spending a significant portion of their time working, they are satisfied with the quality of their college experience, and even indicate levels of involvement in co-curricular life on par with other small, residential institutions where students are working fewer hours. In addition, the university has a respectable retention and graduation rate.

The campus has always been committed to involving students in the campus community. University regulations prescribe that all policy committees (with the exception of the personnel committee) have a minimum of 20% student representation. Many faculty members, particularly those in small departments, rely on advanced undergraduates to help with departmental programming, tutoring, and teaching assistance. A joint initiative between the provost's and Student Life offices formalized the significance of students working on campus when discretionary funds were used to create more meaningful learning experiences through campus employment. Faculty and administrative offices applied for the funds by submitting position descriptions. These positions are periodically reviewed by a university committee to ensure that they provide students educationally relevant work experience. As a result, undergraduates serve as research assistants, campus photographers and landscapers, and directors of community service and fitness programs. Currently, more than one third

of the SU students are employed on campus in jobs that at many institu-
tions are staffed by full-time employees.

The high involvement of students as employees yields significant
benefits for all students. A large number of students show up for campus
events, including major concerts, parties, lectures, and poetry readings.
The Friday night coffeehouse featuring SU student talent draws a few
hundred students each week. Most of this programming is created and
delivered by students with student affairs professionals providing con-
siderable support to student leadership development. For example, resi-
dence life professionals developed a training program to teach resident
assistants and student leaders in campus activities how to collaborate on
events, maximize resources, develop interactive educational program-
ming, and promote programs. In addition, SU students and student
affairs professionals, particularly Financial Aid and Career Service
Center staff, work closely with interested faculty members involved in
local community service. The collaborative goal is to increase student par-
ticipation in existing community initiatives. These initiatives expanded
after SU took full advantage of funds through the Community Service
Federal Work-Study program, in which students with work-study
awards are employed in community service organizations. This effort
also increased the number of student coordinators of campus-community
partnerships.

In this vignette, student involvement and leadership are core operating principles. In the student-driven model, the focus is on developing
students' capacity as leaders and valuing students as integral members
of the university community. Students drive campus activities and are
involved at high levels in co-curricular life. The institution has organized itself through university policy mandating student membership
on committees, in the allocation of discretionary funds, and employment for significant numbers of students. These initiatives promote
meaningful involvement of students across various levels of the
institution.

Although most student affairs units support the concept of
student involvement, the student-driven model takes involvement a
step beyond to something more akin to student investment. The student-
driven model strategically and purposefully builds student involvement in salient campus activities. Students on campuses embracing the

student-driven model hire or involve students voluntarily in activities normally reserved for full-time staff: building design and planning, program management and delivery, and committee leadership.

The student-driven model capitalizes on student talent and leadership. Using talented students in paraprofessional roles has long been encouraged in student affairs (Winston & Ender, 1988). But in the student-driven model, paraprofessionals are effectively used in a variety of settings customarily reserved for full-time student affairs professionals. These areas include academic advising, tutoring, counseling, health education, career development and placement, admissions, drug and alcohol education, community service and volunteer coordination, and recreation programs. The student-driven model relies on students' talents and investment in the institution.

Through meaningful campus work experiences, students become vested members of the campus community. They take the initiative and responsibility to positively contribute to campus and community life as well as assume greater responsibility for the quality of the undergraduate program.

History and Theoretical Foundation of the Student-Driven Model

In the mid-1800s, U.S. colleges were profoundly transformed by the actions of undergraduate students. Students established activities, including literary societies and fraternities, which added a new vitality to campus life. According to Rudolph (1990), "the vigor of the extra-curriculum was proof that the undergraduates had succeeded in assuming significant authority over college life" (p. 156). The history of U.S. higher education attests to the fact that these early organizations quickly became an expected part of campus life (Horowitz, 1987). The student-driven model is a continuation of student authority in and responsibility for campus life.

Student Involvement Theory. Astin's (1984) involvement theory is a guiding framework for the student-driven model for student affairs practice. This theory proposes that the amount of physical and psychological energy that a student devotes to the academic experience is positively related to the impact of college on the student (1977,

1993). Pascarella and Terenzini (1991, p. 50) summarized A.W. Astin's student involvement theory as follows:

> His [Astin's] theory "can be stated simply: *Students learn by becoming involved.*" He sees in his theory elements of the Freudian notion of cathexis (the investment of psychological energy), as well [as] the learning theory concept of time-on-task. He suggests five "basic postulates": (1) involvement requires the investment of psychological and physical energy in "objects" (for example, tasks, people, activities) of one sort or another, whether specific or highly general; (2) involvement is a continuous concept—different students will invest varying amounts of energy in different objects; (3) involvement has both quantitative and qualitative features; (4) the amount of learning or development is directly proportional to the quality and quantity of involvement; and (5) educational effectiveness of any policy or practice is related to its capacity to induce student involvement. (Astin, 1985, pp. 135–136)

The student-driven model exemplifies the crux of the involvement theory in that the more a student is involved in the college or university experience, the more positive outcomes accrue (Astin 1977, 1993; Pascarella & Terenzini, 2005). Through involvement, students benefit from positive interactions with their peers as well as frequent, meaningful interactions with faculty and other adults on campus.

Student Engagement. Growing from student involvement theory is student engagement theory. Student engagement has two key components that contribute to student success. The first is the amount of time and effort students put into their studies and other activities that lead to the experiences and outcomes that constitute student success. The second is the ways that the institution allocates resources and organizes learning opportunities and services to induce students to participate in and benefit from such activities (Kuh et al., 2005, p. 9).

> Student engagement, therefore, is a joint effort between the student and the institution. Students must be prepared to be actively involved and engaged in campus life. But, institutions must marshal their resources, shape their environment and facilities, determine

their policies, and plan their services and programs in ways that encourage student involvement. Neither party, student, nor institution can achieve the learning potential of student engagement separately. (Kuh et al., 2005, p. 9)

A major principle of student engagement is fulfilled in the student-driven model in that the institution channels students' energies into the activities that research shows contribute to student learning and development. In the institution profiled in the vignette above, campus leaders intentionally decreased the number of students working off campus by increasing the number and quality of campus jobs. Since research finds that students who work on campus are more likely to persist (Pascarella & Terenzini, 2005), meaningful campus work experiences have significant educational benefits. Students gain opportunities to apply what they are learning to practical, real-life situations and prepare them for employment after graduation. Therefore, campus employment opportunities were strategically used to increase student engagement and success.

Mattering. Schlossberg's "Marginality and Mattering" (1989) lends theoretical strength to the student-driven model. Schlossberg theorized that the more students feel that their efforts are needed and appreciated, the more they feel like they matter. Mattering is expressed by faculty and administrators and felt by students when students are invited to lend their expertise to efforts, paid or volunteer, that acknowledge their talents. When their sense of responsibility and achievement is engaged and perspectives valued, mattering occurs. Although Schlossberg saw mattering as a precursor to students' involvement, when students know that they matter within a community, involvement and engagement in college life are sustained.

Retention and Integration. Congruent with the concept of student involvement, student engagement, and mattering, Tinto's (1993) theory of integration suggests that involvement in the institution—both academic and social—is critical for student success and persistence. The theory explains that students are influenced by interactions with the structures and members of the academic and social systems of the institution. The more students are integrated into the institution, the more likely they will remain enrolled. This theory is enacted through the student-driven model when students identify strongly with the culture, purposes, and goals of the institution. The student-driven model cultivates students' identification with the institution and such identification leads to increased student retention (Tinto, 1993).

Strengths of the Student-Driven Model

The primary strength of the student-driven model is that it enriches student learning outside the classroom. Students who formed the early literary societies and fraternities recognized the potential of out-of-classroom learning. In fact, the literary societies were founded because of student disappointment with the in-class academic experience (Rudolph, 1990). But it is not only the students directly involved with out-of-classroom experiences or campus employment who benefit from gains in involvement and student engagement. A finding of the DEEP institutions, certainly reflected in decades of student affairs work, was that students are better able to draw their peers into educationally purposeful activities. Although student affairs educators provide the structure, encouragement, and supervision required for successful student involvement, this highly involved and deeply implicated strategy of paraprofessional involvement yields tremendous gains for all students.

A second benefit of the student-driven model is that while students' high levels of institutional investment advantages students in terms of leadership experience and meaningful connections, the institution also benefits in increased retention rates and an enriched quality of student life. The student-driven model yields strong student ownership of university programming and services. In this model, students' contributions to campus life are recognized and highly valued by campus leaders. As one student affairs paraprofessional at a DEEP school stated, "The university needs students to operate." Another described the institution as a "nonprofit organization . . . its success depends on volunteers" (Kuh et al., 2005, p. 150).

This model offers a way for an underresourced institution to reframe a financial necessity into an educationally empowering experience. Not only do paraprofessionals stretch precious institutional resources further to reach more students, but these campus employees greatly benefit from the experience. For example, tutors usually learn as much or more about the respective subject than those they tutor (Pascarella & Terenzini, 1991, 2005).

Paraprofessionals enable expanded services otherwise not available on a resource-limited campus. More important, their involvement encourages community affiliation. Student-driven models cultivate a strong sense of identification between the student and the institution. The student gains a belief that they matter. Through the paraprofessionals' involvement as leaders and campus staff members, their peers benefit from the caring, mattering environment created. This learning climate fosters student retention and satisfaction as well as a rich educational experience.

Faculty members and administrators also benefit from working with paraprofessionals. For example, at one DEEP institution, upper-class student preceptors were paired with faculty members teaching in the first-year curriculum. The preceptors were responsible for co-creating the course and assignments with the faculty member, coordinating co-curricular learning experiences, and mentoring new students. The faculty in these courses learned from preceptors how undergraduates today respond to class assignments and activities as well as how to modify policies to encourage a desired effect on student behavior. Most important, perhaps, preceptors provided new ideas about how to improve the course and faculty members' teaching. Indeed, faculty at many DEEP schools told us that working with a preceptor or peer tutor renewed and deepened their enthusiasm for teaching.

Weaknesses of the Student-Driven Model

Involvement theory and the related concepts of student engagement, mattering, and integration that define the student-driven model work well in most college settings with traditional students. However, the model does not as easily adapt to the realities of college students and institutions today. For example, students historically underrepresented in higher education in general and at specific institutions might find it hard to get involved to the degree expected of the student-driven model. The power of tradition among the student body at some institutions may squelch the involvement of students who may not see themselves reflected in the activities and programming events. While the most traditional form of the student-driven model contains these faults, one can easily see how adaptations of the model can increase its relevance and applicability to current students. Although students today represent a wider range of ages, economic backgrounds, educational preparation, and other diverse characteristics than ever before, the model has great salience for student affairs educators who use the principles of the model yet adopt its traditional application. The DEEP research shows that all students, to varying degrees, desire a rich learning experience. Although the traditional approaches to leadership involvement may not fit all who student affairs educators wish to reach, the student-driven model, with adaptations, has the potential to shape a learning climate that touches all students to a certain extent. In fact, this abundance of learning opportunities was another characteristic of the DEEP project schools and a reason for the higher than predicted student engagement.

Employing students as paraprofessionals has its challenges. As Frigault, Maloney, and Trevino (1986) suggest, student affairs divisions implementing a paraprofessional program must be aware of the increased demands it will place on the staff. Paraprofessionals provide additional staff resources, but they also increase staff responsibilities with respect to training and supervision. Benedict, Casper, Larson, Littlepage, and Panke (2000) noted challenges associated with peer paraprofessional programs, including the loss of students during the training process, lack of fit between students' academic life and office pressures, danger of asking too much of these students, limitations on their time schedule due to class conflicts, time and money necessary to do these programs well, and competition between nonpaid and paid positions.

In the end, the challenge associated with adopting a student-driven model is not one of recognizing and utilizing student talents. It is one of effectively and efficiently managing the approach so that student success is enhanced. The commitment to deliberately and strategically employing paraprofessionals through the adoption of a student-driven model entails, to some extent, relinquishing some control and power. Student affairs divisions considering this approach must decide how willing they are to bestow this level of trust and confidence in their students.

Student Agency Model

The third model discussed in this chapter on student-centered innovative student affairs models is the student agency model. This model advances several steps beyond the student-driven model such that students are completely responsible for student life and perform as full, equal partners with faculty and staff in these efforts.

> *Warren College [a pseudonym] is a small, mostly residential campus community with a clear sense of purpose, coherent values, and a collegial atmosphere. Students, faculty, and staff share a philosophical obligation to make the college an intense, empowering educational experience as well as further ideals of civic engagement and social responsibility. An unusual and functional egalitarianism and a special level of caring and community are distinctive qualities of the college. From the first week on campus, almost all students get involved in something. The institution instills in its students a sense of collective responsibility for operating important areas of the campus. Students tutor peers at the Writing Center, plan major events, enforce the honor code, serve on institutional committees and task forces, and hold approximately 700 leadership roles in clubs and organizations.*
>
> *The institution's honor code is a focal point for socializing students to the Warren culture. Students talk about the Honor Code Rule with respect. A senior said, "Warren gives you the freedom to make mistakes and learn from them. You're accountable to your peers and you learn to trust each other." Equally important, students hold each other accountable. Thus, some of the important lessons students learn are not from books or classroom discussions but from being held accountable and taking responsibility for their actions. New students hear about it long before they matriculate. After they arrive, upper-division students inform newcomers what is acceptable and what is not. The honor code orienteers (HCOs) oversee new students' introduction to the code. They facilitate discussions of Honor Code issues and serve as resources for students and faculty.*

It's nearing the end of the fall term and the Warren First Year Core Council, a committee of students, faculty, and student affairs adminis-trators, are meeting to finalize decisions on the proposals for next year's first-year seminar topics as well as discuss new students' orientation to the Honor Code. The committee is co-chaired by the director of First Year Experience and a junior. The junior convenes the meeting and the group quickly decides on topics based mostly on input from students. Students then champion the adoption of a theme for the first-year experience to integrate the activities associated with the course and co-curricular activi-ties. A sophomore and a student affairs staff member agree to chair the subcommittee to develop components of the theme. Next, the committee discusses ways that the HCOs can have a greater role in helping students develop community standards for their residence hall floors.

History and Philosophy of the Student Agency Model

Bandura (2001) defined the concept of personal agency as the capac-ity to exercise control over the nature and quality of one's life. To be an agent is to intentionally make things happen by one's actions. The core features of agency enable students to play a role in their self-development and learning. The word "agency" is thoroughly and vigor-ously discussed in sociological theory. Giddens (1979), in particular, is a proponent of agency and its relationship to structure and power. According to Giddens, "'action' or agency . . . does not refer to a series of discrete acts combined together, but to *a continuous flow of conduct*" (1979, p. 55). Most relevant to the student agency model is the idea that human beings are conscious agents of their actions. Human agents—in other words, students—monitor and rationalize their activities to make intentional, aware choices. This approach is in stark contrast to pater-nalistic approaches, which consider students as either irrational actors who sometimes make unintentional and ill-informed choices or actors not to be trusted to make their own choices. Theories of agency, on the contrary, state that all humans have some degree of consciousness about the choices they make.

When students are acknowledged as knowing, aware actors, they become empowered, active, and invested in their education. Student empowerment occurs when a climate is created and mechanisms enacted through which students *want* to be responsible for their educa-tion. They are agents of their learning process. Student affairs practice in a student agency model utilizes a hands-off, rather than hands-on, approach to student success. Extremely high expectations communicated prior to admission through a process of anticipatory socialization set the tone that students are responsible for the educational climate. In fact,

> when student agents are left . . . on their own (without influence from professional staff), they are empowered by the ability to come to their own intentionally driven actions. Initiative results from their ability to make personal/group conclusions on what goals and decisions are important. (R. Jeep, personal communication, April 2005)

Because faculty and administrators create structures that empower rather than limit, students take ownership for and become invested in creating, learning, and sharing knowledge. Rather than planning and implementing activities based on individual student needs as in the ethic of care model, the student agency model requires student affairs professionals to empower students as a whole to take initiative. For instance, using this model, student affairs units create policies and structures to facilitate student involvement. They provide training and support to student leaders to enable their efforts. But in the end, the activities, decisions, and programs are the responsibility of students.

The vignette above provides a glimpse of how Warren College cultivates student empowerment through its egalitarian philosophy and belief in highly involved student participation. The belief in students' capacity as human empowered agents is a core assumption of the student agency model. Student initiative is encouraged and high expectations for student participation in decision making and governance are set. Vastly different from the models for practice where administrators are central, students are the primary agents of the learning process. Student affairs administrators have important roles to play, but it is helpful to think of these roles more as guides or facilitators, not the central actors. The student agency model is the student-centered model that likely feels most unfamiliar to the student affairs field. Student affairs professionals who are accustomed to exerting control over students will find that there is little tolerance for intrusive administrators in this model.

The student agency model is predominantly found in colleges and universities with missions and philosophies rooted in the liberal arts. The model works well in institutions that are iconoclastic, innovative, or experimental. These institutions expect students to assume as much responsibility as possible for their education and recognize that a student agency approach to student affairs is central to this goal.

Although the principles of student agency were fostered to some degree at all of the educationally effective colleges in the DEEP project, several student affairs units extensively employed this approach to facilitate student engagement and success. In these instances, academic and co-curricular programs are organized to foster substantial student commitment and accountability. For example, at one DEEP school, students are required to take charge of their learning by contributing to course development. Faculty list course proposals on the specified bulletin boards in the library building; students add their ideas and comment on those suggested by faculty. As such, the shape of the final course is a collaborative effort of students and faculty who are all considered "co-learners" in the educational process. Students are expected to advise deans and faculty about the overall shape, scope, and content of the curriculum.

Shared governance and student involvement in decision making are other central features of the student agency model. Campus governance structures and processes depend on student participation and leadership. Although most student affairs divisions involve students on committees, in a student agency approach, administrators go beyond simply seeking student input and views; significant aspects of the governance process are their responsibility. Governance is a true collaboration among equal students, faculty, and administrators. A student leader at a DEEP school that embraced this philosophy told us, "The committee I was on was selecting an architect. I didn't like the designs of one of the firms and we spent two hours talking about my concerns." Another student added, "They see us as equals. My vote counted just as much as the faculty's. . . . They know this is our school and they want to know how we want the university to be run" (Kuh et al., 2005, p. 169). In return for taking responsibility, the learning environment is extremely rich.

There were several additional examples of student agency at DEEP institutions. At the University of Kansas,

> over the years the Student Senate has been responsible for initiating a number of major programs including the Center for Community Outreach (CCO) and the Multicultural Resource Center—both of which would not be in existence had it not been for student initiative and a "take charge" attitude. During various student interviews, students commented on the encouragement they received from administrators and faculty to "take initiative" and be responsible for various aspects of their undergraduate experience. This, in turn, results in a great deal of "student empowerment" that leads to higher levels of involvement in a range of institutional activities. (NSSE, 2004c, p. 31)

At Evergreen State University in Washington, one of the

> founding values was innovation and the rejection of its opposite—"standardization." This way the College could stay free of the usual (and too often ineffective) academic routines in favor of working collegially, of helping students take responsibility for their own education, and of affording students the freedom to grow with the minimum of intellectual prescription or restraint. Instead they have developed an effective pedagogy marked by individual responsibility for learning coupled with attention and nurturance by the faculty. (National Survey of Student Engagement, 2004b, p. 9)

This innovation and freedom is matched in the approach to student affairs practice where students are full partners, not merely advisors or observers. Evergreen is, perhaps, the most notable example of the student agency model.

The notion of giving students voice and choice in their educational life has roots in the work of John Dewey (1916, 1940) and the progressive movement in education. Dewey advocated that education should encourage students to function as members of a community, actively pursuing interests in cooperation with others. This process of self-directed learning guided by educators best prepares students for the demands of responsible membership within a democratic community.

Student empowerment took on greater significance in education through the influential work of Paulo Freire (1985), who believed that education has the potential to empower students by instilling in them "critical consciousness," or the ability to perceive social, political, and economic oppression and to take action against the oppressive elements of society. Students empower themselves by taking responsibility for their own learning (actively engaging as teachers as well as students), by increasing their understanding of the communities in which they live, and by understanding how they as individuals are affected by current and potential policies and structures. Student empowerment models are grounded in social transformation and pluralism. These models often frame awareness programs and other social justice activities to promote awareness of oppression and social justice. Educators using a student agency model must be willing to challenge deeply held assumptions about power, social justice, and other conventions about education.

Although educational philosophies of empowerment typically focus on social purposes of empowerment, including working toward democracy and social transformation, Lawrence Lightfoot (1986) defined empowerment as "the opportunity a person has for autonomy, responsibility, choice, and authority" (p. 9). This view attaches a personal emphasis on the development of an individual's sense of agency in education. In keeping with the goals of democracy and community involvement, the student agency model is closely aligned with the principles of social action and service learning. As students complete service learning projects with a deeper sense of meaning about what they are learning, they also see more clearly and appreciate the connections between the university and community.

Strengths of the Student Agency Model

To empower students is to give them a share in the movement and direction of the educational enterprise. When students perceive that they are responsible for the quality of their educational experience, they are likely to feel invested in their learning and success. A student at one of the DEEP schools stated it plainly: "Students are so empowered here to be engaged. We truly have ownership of our lives and so we just assume we'll be in charge of things. It's amazing how motivated that makes you to take on responsibility and succeed" (Kuh et al., 2005, p. 2). Student affairs professionals who are able to increase student involvement in decision making as well as provide students the opportunity to initiate and carry out new ideas create enhanced learning opportunities for students.

Education from a position of student agency teaches students about their rights *and* their responsibilities. This balance not only teaches them how to make decisions and choices that affect their lives but also fosters independence. Engaging students in their own learning by having them be active in and contribute to the campus community enables them to develop autonomy and personal responsibility.

Similar to the student-driven model, the student agency model also relies on student workers to provide a wide range of student services. However, in a student agency model, this involvement is focused on students' contributions as educators. For example, students at DEEP schools with a student agency model serve in important roles as tutors and peer educators. At one institution, tutors must obtain certification from the College Reading and Learning Association, maintain a cumulative and major grade point average (GPA) of 3.0, and work a certain number of hours per semester. By investing in quality tutoring and peer education training and offering students academic credit for this training, these institutions have legitimized peer teaching as a vehicle for sharing responsibility for student learning. Another institution employs student mentors to assist students with research. A mentee, usually a first-year student, is mentored by a junior or senior who is the primary investigator on the research project. The faculty member overseeing the research project in turn mentors the advanced student. This collaborative model increases the number of students who can participate in a meaningful way in research and connects faculty with both advanced and beginning students.

Weaknesses of the Student Agency Model

The often task-oriented perspective of the student affairs field creates an uncomfortable fit with the student agency model. Certainly, more than one student affairs educator has bemoaned the inefficiency of leaving program and service planning and execution to student initiative.

But, student initiative is what student agency model proponents desire. In this model, programs and services may be inefficient and a bit messy. Students may fulfill their urge to reinvent the system each year or every couple of years. Administrators may find themselves revisiting issues that they would rather put behind them as resolved. This continual making and remaking is central to student agency work. Student affairs educators working within this model must have high tolerances for ambiguity and reiteration.

The student agency model would, most likely, be incongruent on campuses with high involvement of external stakeholders such as parents and legislators. These external participants in campus life often expect a level of professionalism and service not afforded by the student agency model. This type of education (often featuring trial by error or tolerance of learning through mistakes) would, most likely, not appear to be efficient to these important constituents. In a consumer environment, where highly polished and crisply delivered services and programs are expected, the student agency model would fall short.

In the student agency model, students are expected to examine situations critically and make thoughtful, well-informed decisions. However, as more than one student affairs administrator at DEEP schools with this model told us, "students struggle with the tension between freedom and responsibility and with the absence of clearly defined limits sometimes they screw up" (Kuh et al., 2005, p. 123). Indeed, the student agency perspective views students making mistakes as an important part of their learning.

Conclusion

Often in student affairs, our efforts are invisible if, through pro-action, problems are averted and students thrive in intentionally designed environments. In the student agency model, mistakes and errors readily occur. The inherent messiness of this model is evident for all to see. Therefore, how might one assess educational progress and achievement in the student agency model? How is educational success measured in the student agency model? Engagement and process are key elements in determining success in the student agency model.

Several DEEP institutions and their success in higher than predicted student engagement and graduation rates speak to the power of the student agency model. Certainly, this is not a model for all schools. In fact, there may be very few schools able to carry out this model effectively. But, as an innovative approach focusing on student empowerment and initiative, perhaps more schools could benefit from a consideration of its principles and philosophy.

CHAPTER 7

ACADEMIC AND COLLABORATION INNOVATIVE MODELS

Collaboration between academic and student affairs has received considerable encouragement since the publication of *Powerful Partnerships* (AAHE et al., 1998). The partnership has been furthered through the proliferation of learning communities, service learning, first-year experience programs, and other initiatives dependent on cooperation between student and academic affairs (Sandeen, 2004). Although improved institutional effectiveness and administrative functioning are often behind the formation of student and academic affairs partnerships (Martin & Murphy, 2000; Schroeder, 1999a), the most significant rationale for such collaboration is enhancing student learning and success (Garland & Grace, 1993; Schroeder, 1999b; Schuh, 1999).

Indeed, the rich histories and traditions of student and academic affairs offer complementary strengths to support student learning and development (Price, 1999). A focus on student success creates even more impetus for collaboration. According to Guarasci (2001), absent an alliance between academic and student affairs, an institution is only minimally supporting student success.

Colleges and universities that exemplify linked academic and student affairs divisions place student learning at the center of their joint enterprise and create institutional coherence about student success. Unlike the learning-centered models described in chapter 5 and in which academic affairs and student affairs stake out separate domains concerning their contributions to student success, the more innovative academic and collaborative models discovered at several DEEP schools emphasize mutual territory and combined efforts to engender student engagement and success.

Educationally effective models for student affairs practice that emphasize academic collaboration are in step with the educational mission, and work to promote student learning outcomes. At several DEEP colleges, student affairs staff work in partnership with academic affairs and other institutional support structures to an impressive degree (Kinzie & Kuh, 2004; Kuh et al., 2005). In this chapter, two innovative approaches to student affairs practice that emphasize collaboration around the academic mission are described. The first model, academic-student affairs collaboration, features a tightly coupled student affairs–academic affairs structure and operational philosophy discussed extensively in student affairs literature. This model emphasizes seamless collaboration between student and academic affairs. The second approach, academic centered, is organized around the academic core and wholeheartedly privileges academic experiences over more traditional co-curricular activities common to student affairs. In this second model, student affairs is highly responsive to the rigors of the curriculum, providing structural support in an intense academic environment. These two models were more likely to be found at the selective institutions studied in the DEEP project. However, because the features of these models were exemplified at most of the DEEP project schools, it is likely that they are strongly associated with student success.

Academic-Student Affairs Collaboration Model

The director of student leadership programs at Manchester University [a pseudonym] is reviewing new senior capstone experience proposals for one of her main committee assignments on the Council for Liberal Education. The proposals were submitted by academic departments for the purpose of enhancing the integration of co-curricular and applied learning experiences in the required senior culminating course. The director, who championed this revision, created a rubric for committee members to evaluate the degree to which co-curricular experiences are knit into the proposed seminars. Co-curricular leadership has always been a highlight of the student experience at Manchester, and the infusion of applied leadership experiences in the capstone course has created a rich learning experience for seniors.

Earlier this fall the director worked with a small group of faculty and student affairs staff to design approaches to assess student learning outcomes, such as learning independently, working effectively with, and contributing to the welfare of others. She's also been working with faculty members in business and sociology to increase the theoretical links between student activities programming related to service and leadership. Assessment data show that student learning is enhanced through the combined theoretical and applied structure.

Over the past 10 years, student affairs has been more intentional about enhancing the connections between programming and the academic mission of the institution. For example, residence life staff and faculty worked jointly to develop theme floors in the residence halls to increase the promotion of educational mission objectives concerning multiculturalism, the arts, and service. Faculty members' involvement in programming conducted through the student activities and residence life has also increased. The director of student leadership understands that her work is best achieved through working collaboratively with faculty and staff on the Council for Liberal Education and in other aspects of campus life. Although she still does a significant amount of leadership programming in student affairs, she recognizes that her work is more educationally effective when it is closely tied to the academic mission.

Now I see that my work is about finding opportunities for collaboration with other academic departments and faculty. It requires me to fully understand academic culture and to orient my work around the educational mission of the institution. At first I worried that I was giving up territory, but now I see that more can be accomplished in the name of student learning when student and academic affairs work together.

This depiction of student affairs work through the perspective of the director of student leadership at Manchester University is typical of the academic-student affairs collaboration model of student affairs practice. This model emphasizes significant interactions between student and academic affairs staff around the common purpose of enhanced student learning. Student affairs and academic affairs maintain most of their distinct functions, but capitalize on the strengths of their standpoints. For example, the director of student leadership used her extensive knowledge of leadership development during the creation of an applied leadership experience in the senior capstone course. In similar fashion, faculty members joined residence life staff in the creation of academic enrichment programming on theme floors to increase the educational potential of the residence halls.

In this model, student affairs professionals and faculty members appreciate each other's respective strengths and join together to facilitate the educational mission. Although separate spheres of expertise are respected, the aim is to blur the boundaries between the domains. For example, in the opening vignette, the collaboration among those within the council on liberal education is a reflection of seamless learning, in which the enhancement of student learning and creation of effective learning environments is a shared responsibility. This perspective is advanced through a committee that includes a balanced representation of faculty and student affairs professionals.

Powerful partnerships result when the contributions and talents of academic and student affairs are combined to promote student success. The relationship between student and academic affairs is reciprocal in that they are regularly involved in each other's primary areas. At several DEEP project schools, a shared focus on student success fostered this involvement and partnership. For example, one of the DEEP schools combined orientation, advising, learning communities, and academic support functions into a university college unit in academic affairs. The VPSA within this institution expressed the importance of maintaining an unwavering focus on student success as the goal, even after student advising programs were moved from student affairs to academic affairs:

"I gave up designs about territory long ago. Yes, one might look at this move as a loss for student affairs, but now we are better partners working to support students" (Kuh et al., 2005, p. 167). The vice president's collaborative mindset was central to ensuring an effective university college program.

History and Philosophy of the Academic–Student Affairs Collaboration Model

In recent years, the call for student and academic affairs collaboration has been connected to advanced discussions about the key role student affairs professionals play in the student learning process. The leading student affairs professional associations including the ACPA and the NASPA advocated the importance of collaboration between student affairs and academic affairs and proposed models for creating a learning environment on campus. *The Student Learning Imperative*, published by ACPA in 1996, championed a joint commitment to student learning. However, in the early 1990s, the collaboration was perceived to be rather one sided, with the major emphasis being to involve faculty in student affairs programming, and with little reciprocal involvement of student affairs in the academic arena. In addition, Bourassa and Kruger (2001) indicated there was little evidence of a comparable movement among academic affairs organizations. Despite this initial lack of correspondence, over the next several years the collaboration evolved to a more complex, campus-wide perspective requiring parallel commitments by faculty and student affairs staff.

Although the focus on student learning and simultaneous emphasis on collaboration with academic affairs captured the attention of student affairs since 1994, Roberts (1998) posited that student learning as a cooperative effort among campus community members began with the ACE's *Student Personnel Point of View, 1937*. The statement was intended as a philosophy to be adopted by faculty and administrators. It specified that institutions should encourage the cooperation of all campus members, including faculty, administrators, and students, in an effort to create effective learning environments. Despite this early focus on collaboration, the emphasis was soon undermined with the creation of *The Student Personnel Point of View, 1949* revision that distinguished separate roles for student affairs staff and faculty, and effectively established functional areas in student affairs (Roberts, 1998). The *Student Learning Imperative* (ACPA, 1996) and other national position statements advocating institutional partnerships in effect renewed the philosophy of the original *Student Personnel Point of View* by advocating for student and academic affairs collaboration.

Research on the impact of college on students provides further support for the academic-student affairs collaboration model. When student and academic affairs join their efforts, students have increased opportunities for learning since in- and out-of-classroom activities are structured to build upon each other (Kezar, 2003b; Schroeder & Hurst, 1996). Given that student learning is enhanced through mutually reinforcing educational experiences in and out of the classroom (Pascarella & Terenzini, 2005), it seems that the academic-student affairs collaboration model is more likely to produce powerful learning environments and student success. A focus on learning in separate student and academic spheres diminishes these gains.

The guiding philosophy of the academic-student affairs collaboration model is the belief that student learning transcends administrative hierarchies and functional area boundaries. True collaboration between student and academic affairs is based in a tightly coupled system in which units deepen their understanding of the other's culture as well as appreciate the other's talents to create effective learning environments. Successful collaborative ventures are based in a trust that cooperation will not reduce the importance of, or result in a loss of territory for, either collaborator. Instead, the collaboration creates improved environments for all members of the campus community, particularly students.

Features of the Academic-Student Affairs Collaboration Model
The academic-student affairs collaboration model emphasizes the shared relationship between all campus entities as well as the importance of developing a mutual agenda concerning student success.

Student Affairs as a Partner in the Learning Enterprise. The ability to collaborate depends on the belief that all parties are equally vital to the enterprise of student learning. For example, at one DEEP school with a strong academic-student affairs collaboration model, the words "collaboration" and "partnerships" were used by faculty, administrators, and students to describe the relationship among campus community members. This perspective reflected a shared vision held by senior academic and student affairs leaders of what the institution can and should be in relationship to the undergraduate experience. Most important, this approach works because the student affairs professionals understand that their fundamental mission is the intellectual mission of the university. Also important, student life programs and policies emphasize intellectual growth and challenge, often considered the domain of faculty. As a result, collaboration with academic affairs is a high priority and a guiding operating principle.

In contrast to the rhetoric portraying student affairs as secondary to the educational mission—or worse, inferior to academic affairs—the dialogue in the academic-student affairs collaboration model depicts student affairs as a full partner in the learning enterprise. Student affairs practitioners see themselves making significant contributions to student learning both in and out of the classroom. The emphasis on the educational mission and partnership with faculty also enables a creative and challenging work environment for student affairs professionals. Much like the director of student leadership in the opening vignette, student affairs staff members find novel opportunities to connect their work to the academic enterprise. Moreover, because student success can only be accomplished through the work of multiple functional areas, the educational role of student affairs is ensured.

Student and Academic Affairs as Tightly Coupled. Organizational theorists refer to the relationships between parts of organizations as "couplings." Coupling refers to the degree to which one component of the system influences, and is influenced by, other components. Weick (1976) is the theorist most closely identified with coupling in educational organizations. His definition is based on the number of variables shared between two separate entities. Coupling may be "tight" or "loose" according to the importance and commonality of variables. Two parts of a system are said to be tightly coupled if they have a great influence on each other. At educationally effective colleges and universities with a strong collaborative model, student and academic affairs are tightly coupled.

The units share the common purpose of fostering student learning and unite around the educational mission.

For the collaborative model to be effective, key players in student and academic affairs must be frequently brought together. Collaborative relationships develop and are enhanced through personal contacts. More important, student and academic affairs staff must have the capacity to influence each other. For example, at one DEEP school, faculty members concerned about first-year students' infrequent experiences with active and collaborative learning recognized that it was not enough to focus on improvements to teaching in the first-year seminar. Instead, they formed a committee of student affairs staff, faculty, students, and librarians to implement an enriched first-year program. The committee was encouraged by support from the dean of students and dean of the college, who pooled resources to create innovative curricular and co-curricular programming. Student affairs staff refined the programmatic aspects of the reconfigured program, including linking resident assistants and the first-year seminar, introducing the program to new students at orientation, and supporting experiential activities. The success of this initiative demonstrates the benefits of tight coupling between student and academic affairs.

Structural Bridges Link Student and Academic Affairs. The importance of tight coupling in the collaboration model implies high levels of interaction between student affairs and academic affairs. For this to occur, structures must be in place to facilitate linkages among units. For example, at some DEEP institutions, student and academic affairs functional areas were restructured to share reporting lines. At one DEEP school, the VPSA reports directly to the provost and serves on the tenure committee. This ensures that students' out-of-class experiences are represented by student affairs during meetings of the academic deans. This in turn resulted in increased awareness of the educational value of faculty involvement in student affairs programs as well as a higher degree of faculty participation across the board.

At another DEEP institution, reporting lines were modified only in the areas in which collaboration between student affairs and academic affairs was most important. For example, because the university desired a strong partnership around community service and service learning, the community service center in student affairs was reconfigured to jointly report to the provost and VPSA. This structural change can result in clearer philosophical and pedagogical goals, stronger program delivery, increased institutional support, and enhanced student learning. Although some DEEP institutions altered organizational structures to achieve collaboration, other DEEP institutions maintained distinct reporting lines for student and academic affairs and used institutional committees with balanced representation of faculty and student affairs staff as the connection between the two areas. Successful collaboration requires several structural links to bridge the typical organizational boundaries and barriers between academic and student affairs.

Shared Educational Mission and Language Concerning Student Learning and Success. The academic-student affairs collaboration model is effective when the student affairs mission statement fully complements and coincides with the institution's academic mission. Student affairs units that embrace the academic mission and delineate learning outcomes consistent with the institutional educational philosophy are working in concert, rather than at cross purposes, with academic affairs. At one DEEP school with a strong academic-student affairs collaboration model, selection criteria for resident assistants include an understanding of the university mission. They are expected to convey this educational philosophy to new students as well as perform corresponding programming goals.

Common goals between academic and student affairs open opportunities to develop a shared language around student success. Using language related to the educational mission, student affairs staff members can more effectively expand practices that advance this mission, particularly in terms of student learning outcomes. At some DEEP institutions, position titles and office names were changed to reflect this mission commitment. For example, at one DEEP school, the VPSA title was changed to vice provost for student success. Another DEEP school senior student affairs officer was renamed provost for undergraduate studies and campus life. At educationally effective colleges and universities adhering to an academic-student affairs collaboration model, the educational mission was communicated in language representing the educational core. The value of educationally enriching learning experiences for students was continually emphasized.

Strengths and Weaknesses of the Academic-Student Affairs Collaboration Model

Shared responsibility for student success is a common feature of the DEEP schools (Kuh et al., 2005). However, institutions with an academic-student affairs collaboration model shared responsibility for the educational mission to an impressive degree. As such, this interdependence significantly shaped a high-quality learning environment for undergraduates. In contrast to those at institutions where academic and student affairs compete for students' attention (see chapter 3), student affairs professionals at academic-student affairs collaboration model institutions reported a high degree of satisfaction with their work. This was particularly true if they believed in and understood the integral relationship of student affairs to the educational mission. Other benefits of the model include a team-oriented environment in which creativity is encouraged, increased coherence in the undergraduate program, and the opportunity for student and academic affairs to share costs and resources.

Although the strengths of this model outweigh the weaknesses in terms of engendering student success, some challenges exist. Several DEEP schools with this model found that student affairs offices assumed a greater burden of the responsibility to partner with academic affairs. In such cases, student affairs staff must attend to opportunities for collaboration and are more likely to invite collaboration than be invited by academic affairs. A DEEP school transitioning to an academic-student affairs collaboration model experienced challenges when creating living-learning communities because some student affairs staff members did not understand that faculty involvement and a partnered academic-student affairs focus warranted a transformed operations philosophy. The tension around this initiative exposed the larger issue of lack of understanding and appreciation for differences in student affairs and academic cultures. Magolda (2005) provides some cautions with regard to partnerships, including investigating how the collaboration fits with the partners' views about teaching and learning.

Not all partnerships are virtuous. When student and academic affairs partners do not view themselves as equally vital to student learning, collaborations are lopsided and unfair. One DEEP school with a nascent academic-student affairs collaboration model crafted a limited role for student affairs staff members in their learning communities. The student affairs staff simply envisioned their role as planning the logistics of the experiential trips for the course, including scheduling the vans and arranging lunches. Although these tasks were vital to the success of learning communities and highlight the administrative strong suit of student affairs professionals, they failed to exercise the full educational talents of the staff members. In addition, if partnerships exist around only a few activities or worse, such activities represent only an isolated component of students' experiences, and they could be viewed as little more than diversions from the academic program.

When partnerships are reciprocal and organized around a common educational mission, collaborative models for student affairs practice create improved opportunities for student learning. With an integrated in- and out-of-classroom experience, students spend more time with educators in learning experiences that build upon each other. This integration is educationally and personally beneficial to students because their undergraduate experience is more holistic and coherent. The coherence inherent in the academic-student affairs collaboration model can address the longstanding problem of fragmentation in undergraduate education.

An additional strength of the academic-student affairs collaboration model is the opportunity to extend resources. For example, at one DEEP school, both student and academic affairs fund the center for service learning. Parallel budget lines make the center more affordable to both units as well as strengthen the commitment of student and academic affairs for the center's success. The center received external funding in part due to its strong academic and student learning outcomes perspective. At a second DEEP institution, the director of student leadership and a faculty member were co-principle investigators on a grant to study the educational outcomes of experiential learning. At a third school, the dean of students and a faculty member obtained a grant to evaluate the success of a science-learning community. These projects not only brought additional resources to the institution, but more importantly reinforced the value of student and academic affairs collaboration.

Academic-Centered Model

Late on a Friday afternoon in one of the group study rooms in the library, senior international studies major, Latrease; sociology major juniors Raja, Derek, and Trina; and Dr. Chisholm, a tenured faculty member in the political science department, are meeting to map out the remaining details for the upcoming summit on poverty. The major speakers confirmed their participation, and the planning team is filling out the program with experiential activities and presummit events. They've adopted a global focus for the summit, including a campus display using World Bank statistics on poverty and a panel on global debt facing developing countries. They incorporated a series of local speakers and community service events to engage students in the local dimensions of poverty. Dr. Chisholm, who is involved in the regional chapter of Habitat for Humanity, and Latrease, who volunteers at the community food bank, are taking most of the responsibility for coordinating service events and other experiential activities. Trina reports that three student organizations and the office of multicultural affairs have signed on as co-sponsors.

The summit promises to be a significant campus event. Students have been organizing on the topic of poverty since the beginning of the school year when the author of the book, The Working Poor, came to the campus for convocation. The committee hopes to reinvigorate the heated discussions started in first-year seminar courses. The students become particularly engaged in conversations about socioeconomic status issues among college students. Raja adjourns the meeting at 6 p.m. so that he and Trina have time to get dinner before they meet up with their sociology study group at the local coffeehouse. Dr. Chisholm and Latrease discuss her graduate school plans as they walk to the student center to check out the space reserved for the summit breakout sessions.

This vignette provides a glimpse of the rich educational programming that occurs at Suffolk College (a pseudonym). Students take responsibility for the development of intellectually stimulating programs as well as tackle challenging issues in complex ways. They connect their community service initiatives to entities beyond the campus and work with faculty and administrators to integrate campus activities with their academic work. Students and faculty frequently discuss ideas from courses outside of class, and faculty members are highly involved with students in all aspects of campus life. This high level of engagement creates a vibrant intellectual community. What is noticeably absent from this illustration is any mention of student affairs. Although the director of student activities and the international program office, both in the division of student affairs, are involved in specific aspects of the poverty summit, this event, like many events at Suffolk, is being coordinated primarily by students and faculty.

Suffolk College is an academically intense learning environment. The institution is well known for its rigorous undergraduate program that appeals to academically motivated students, most of whom aspire to graduate or professional school. Students are dedicated to their coursework and devote significant time and energy to studying. But they appreciate the opportunity to explore ideas and participate in social action outside the classroom, and take responsibility for campus programming that enriches the learning community. Classroom experiences, field experiences and internships, international experiences, and diversity are woven into a tapestry that provides robust educational opportunities for Suffolk students.

Although student affairs is almost invisible in the opening vignette, there are many ways that it is directly involved in events like the poverty summit and, more broadly, in creating an intellectually vibrant learning environment. Student affairs staff members worked with students and faculty to assess the need for more group meeting space in the library. Student affairs staff members took the lead in creating enriched study rooms, with the addition of write-on boards and flexible furniture designs. They also worked with library staff to determine study space reservations, extend hours, and support the operation of a student-run juice and coffee bar in the library. The space quickly became a favorite meeting spot of students who were completing group assignments and conducting committee meetings. Student affairs professionals support the academic mission through work with faculty and students to facilitate discussion and reflection sessions in conjunction with community service projects. Furthermore, student affairs is directly involved in guiding and advising students who plan major events. Notably, the student affairs staff is lean. They expend little energy on sponsoring co-curricular programs, and residence hall programs, admittedly infrequent, are left to the resident assistants and floor council members.

The student affairs division at Suffolk employs an academic-centered model of student affairs practice. In this model, student affairs is involved in providing structural support to make rigorous academics work for students. Student affairs professionals help balance, but not distract from, the intensity of the academic environment and facilitate rich educational programming. According to the dean of students at a DEEP school with this model, "The intenseness of your academics is what makes you belong in this community. . . . The culture . . . is built around academic rigor" (NSSE, 2003f, p. 12). In response, student affairs is in tune with the academic culture and organized around supporting and enriching the academic community. In such a pressure cooker–like educational environment, student affairs also plays a role in helping students relax and recreate. For example, residence hall programming frequently focuses on intramurals and organized study breaks. Involvement in an intense educational mission trumps participation in co- or extracurricular activities unrelated to the academic mission.

History and Philosophy of the Academic-Centered Model
In the earliest colleges in U.S. higher education, a president and a few faculty and staff members administered all the tasks required to maintain the institution's existence (Caple, 1996; Rudolph, 1990). The president and faculty members were primarily concerned with academic matters, though they also performed some roles traditionally associated with counseling and guidance and student conduct. Faculty were involved in all aspects of students' lives. Although faculty and students co-created campus life, the primary focus was classroom learning. This early college structure, which was in place through the 1890s, is the foundation of the academic-centered model for student affairs.

As college enrollments expanded, more students with diverse interests attended college, institutions transformed into complex research institutions and faculty attention shifted to research, and a division of labor was needed. The "scientific study of the student" promoted by

William Rainey Harper created specialized student affairs (Caple, 1996). These developments put forth a dualistic structure, with academic affairs being concerned about the classroom and student affairs charged with campus life outside of the classroom. (This fragmentation, specialization, and dual structure are discussed in chapter 3.) As described earlier in the academic-student affairs collaboration model section, *The Student Personnel Point of View* (ACE, 1937, 1949) articulated a strong student affairs commitment to focus on academic and intellectual development. Although early statements of student affairs philosophy reinforce a commitment to the educational role of student affairs, Brown (1972) plainly confirmed that student affairs should join with faculty to invigorate the curriculum and eliminate the extracurricular.

The academic-centered model for student affairs practice also draws from liberal arts education and liberal arts colleges. Liberal arts education is about strengthening the mind across varied topics to make it stronger and more able to grasp ideas and perform intellectual work. Exercising the mind across multiple academic areas in a liberal arts curriculum, the pursuit of self-initiated inquiry, and interaction with faculty are typical features of liberal arts education (Michalak & Robert, 1981). A liberal arts education is available at many institutional types, but liberal arts colleges are perhaps the most pure form. At their core, liberal arts colleges seek to develop intimate learning environments where extensive interaction between faculty and students and among students themselves fosters a community of serious discourse. Small class sizes, an emphasis on individualized instruction, active participation in the campus community, and faculty dedicated to teaching undergraduates represent the foundation of learning at these institutions (Hersh, 1999). These characteristics are the ideal conditions for the academic-centered model for student affairs practice.

Features of the Academic-Centered Model

Like the academic-student affairs collaboration model, the academic-centered model emphasizes shared responsibility for student success. However, features of the academic-centered model place a strong emphasis on the educational mission, creating an intellectual environment, and the role that student affairs plays in supporting and sustaining these goals.

Academic-Centered Models and Small, Liberal Arts Colleges. The academic-centered model is more likely to be found at small, liberal arts colleges or institutions that provide high-quality liberal arts education. At institutions with an academic-centered model for student affairs, expectations about high levels of academic challenge are knit into the fabric of the history and culture of the institution and reinforced via a well-integrated core curriculum. The hallmark of small liberal arts colleges is that they are, on average, more academically challenging than other types of institutions. Student and academic affairs administrators interact more frequently in these institutions, and as a result, are more likely to work cooperatively on initiatives related to the educational mission (Hirt et al., 2004). These characteristics support an Academic-Centered Model.

Student Learning and Educational Enrichment Are Key Objectives for Student Affairs. Students' personal development remains a primary concern for student affairs in the academic-centered model. But, an equally important emphasis is placed on the role student affairs plays in directly supporting student learning and enriching the intellectual community. Student success and academic rigor are of primary importance. As a result, student affairs professionals tend to:

1. Understand and inquire about students' studies and educational goals.
2. Encourage and support an academic environment that emphasizes studying and spending time on academic work.
3. Participate in the academic community by attending events, taking part in intellectual discourse, and facilitating the integration of in- and out-of-class learning and experiences.
4. Collaborate with faculty and students to develop a rich intellectual community.
5. Complement the academic experience through enriched programming and recreational and relaxing opportunities appropriate in an intense academic environment.

By understanding and inquiring about students' academic needs and goals, student affairs professionals in the academic-centered model are more likely to be proactive in identifying and addressing student learning needs. For example, at one DEEP school with an academic-centered model, the student affairs staff is keenly aware of the assignments in the rigorous first-year seminar and other courses that challenge new students. Programming in the residence halls is responsive to students' academic needs and student affairs staff fosters the development of environments conducive to studying and that support time spent on academic work. Equally important, student affairs staff members in academic-centered models are present for campus academic events. They are likely to participate in events like the poverty summit described in the opening vignette. Participation is symbolically important because it communicates appreciation for the academic mission as well as contributes to student affairs practitioners' capacity to address students' needs.

Student and Academic Affairs Share Reporting Lines. Similar to the academic-student affairs collaboration model described earlier, the senior student affairs officer in an academic-centered model likely reports to the senior academic officer and works closely with academic deans and vice presidents. Campus units related to academic support may even be within the scope of student affairs. Although it is common for student affairs to report directly to the provost or dean of the college in small liberal arts colleges, larger DEEP institutions with an academic-centered model frequently had similar reporting lines. For example, student affairs staff members at a DEEP school with several residential colleges reported to both student and academic affairs. This model ensures that attention is paid to the development of a rich intellectual environment within the residential colleges.

Academic-Centered Models Strongly Influenced by an Academic Student Culture. Students at DEEP schools with an academic-centered model of student affairs pull all-nighters and eschew partying to stay in and do homework at least one weekend night. This academic focus allows them to keep up with the level of intensity required to complete the heavy reading load and assignments necessary for the integration of diverse ideas. A student at one DEEP school with an academic-centered model described her college as having an environment that is "friendly" to studying. This is largely due to the academic orientation of students; however, it was furthered by the redesign of campus facilities based on student input. A variety of study options were created for students in libraries, near faculty offices, in residence halls, and the student center. Library study space was designed as if it were a living room, and comfortable chairs in the student center improved the use of these spaces for studying. Furthermore, "amazing" food, lots of natural light, and a coffee bar brought more students—and faculty—into the student center to study and engage in dialogue.

Students at institutions with an academic-centered model share in the promotion of the focus on the educational mission. For example, residence halls at one DEEP school are primarily run by juniors and seniors. Although four full-time live-in staff members provide professional leadership for more than 15 living units housing 1,000 students, a staff of junior and senior resident assistants provides considerable leadership. The resident assistant's primary programming thrust is a series of programs called dialogues. Each resident assistant leads six dialogue programs per year, including such examples as the war on terror as it relates to civil liberties, international diversity compared with domestic diversity, and balancing greed with making a living. However, a heavy calendar of residentially based programming was not viewed by students as a necessary ingredient for a successful residence hall experience. Rather, students view residence hall living as a complementary experience; that is, it is one of many important out-of-class experiences for students at the college.

Strengths and Weaknesses of the Academic-Centered Model

The academic-centered model has several strengths, the first of which is that organizing student affairs around promoting the educational mission clarifies the role of student affairs in undergraduate education. This model is aligned with the growing academic importance of student affairs in the enhancement of student learning. The academic-centered model provides unique opportunities for student affairs professionals to showcase their talents as educators. Student affairs professionals at DEEP schools with academic-centered models were likely to be teaching and serving in roles that contribute directly to the educational mission. Finally, in an era of diminishing resources and greater focus on increasing student-learning outcomes, organizing student affairs around the academic mission can be cost effective. Pooling resources and reducing compartmentalization makes for a focused effort concerning student success.

On the other hand, the prominence of the educational mission in student affairs work exposes several weaknesses of this model. Similar to findings reported by Hirt et al. (2004), some student affairs administrators at DEEP schools with an academic-centered model reported that faculty did not seem to understand or appreciate the work of student affairs. In response, student affairs staff at one DEEP institution presented a program demonstrating the relationship between student development theory and effective pedagogy at the annual faculty development workshop. Student affairs staff members received additional requests to present this to academic departments, leading to an increase in student affairs staff members' perceptions that faculty appreciated their work.

The academic-centered model is dependent on faculty-student interaction outside of the classroom. However, when this element is threatened—as it was at a DEEP institution that increased the emphasis on research in faculty hiring, promotion, and tenure review—the academic-centered model for student affairs practice is endangered. Increasing research productivity strained the long history of student-faculty interaction around campus programming and reduced student-faculty out-of-class interaction to discuss ideas. Students, student affairs professionals, and faculty were all concerned about the impact of this shift on the quality of intellectual life on campus. In response, approaches to address the concerns were devised. But this new emphasis will require constant monitoring to ensure that the quality of student-faculty interaction does not diminish and that faculty are not overworked in attempts to meet both goals.

Conclusion

The academic-centered and academic-student affairs collaboration models are bolstered by increased emphasis on improving undergraduate education (Chickering & Gamson, 1987; Pascarella & Terenzini, 2005; Sandeen, 2004). Support for these models can be found in the research on student engagement that reinforces the importance of high-quality learning environments in which students and faculty enjoy high levels of interaction and students are frequently involved in educationally enriched activities (Kuh, 2001a; Pascarella & Terenzini, 2005; Schroeder, 1999b). These models offer innovative approaches for student affairs to make meaningful contributions to student engagement and success.

These innovative models help foster an environment described by Barr and Tagg (1995) as aligned with the learning paradigm. These models emphasize the creation of "environments and experiences that bring students to discover and construct knowledge for themselves, to make students members of communities of learners that make discoveries and solve problems, . . . and . . . to create a series of ever more powerful learning environments" (p. 15). The potential for these models to create rich academic environments and robust learning experiences in and outside the classroom demonstrates their value to student success.

According to Sandeen (2004), student affairs professionals "should be expected to contribute significantly to the broadened student learning experiences on their campus" (p. 31). When student affairs professionals view their role as making a contribution to student learning, they are more likely to organize around student success. For example, residence hall directors at DEEP schools sought out opportunities to increase the educational potential of the residence halls by creating environments that supported student study time. If campus community members see the classroom and the laboratory as the exclusive domain for student learning, adopting this perspective can be challenging. The challenge of this approach is exacerbated by faculty members with a narrow interpretation of the term "educator." In addition, because new student affairs professionals are primarily trained at research institutions, they may be unaware of student affairs models with a strong academic focus that require them to work collaboratively with all campus constituents.

The academic-student affairs collaboration and academic-centered models share the perspective that student affairs is an integral component of the academic program in undergraduate education. The models are underscored with the belief that student affairs makes a significant contribution to student learning and success. The models share a common history and philosophy but differ on the degree to which the educational mission is at the core of their work. Whereas the essence of the academic-student affairs collaboration model is on the quality of the partnership between student and academic affairs and the nexus for this collaboration is student learning, the intense focus on supporting the educational mission featured in the academic-centered model can downplay student affairs contributions to student learning.

Both models illustrate the value of making student learning the center of the student affairs enterprise. However, the academic-student affairs collaboration model is more clearly an expression of the partnership theme in student affairs, while the academic-centered model is more likely a response to a robust undergraduate environment. These models have prompted some administrative reshuffling, so that student affairs reports to the provost's or chief academic affairs office. Such arrangements are likely to enhance student learning, particularly when there is a genuine commitment from the provost, academic deans, and faculty to an enriched view of undergraduate education. Although these models have their strengths and weaknesses, their features have profound implications for student affairs practice in an era focused on increasing student success.

PART IV

WEAVING THE BASKET: PUTTING IT ALL TOGETHER

CHAPTER 8

COLLABORATION, STUDENT ENGAGEMENT, AND THE FUTURE OF STUDENT AFFAIRS PRACTICE

Higher education is in the throes of a major transformation. Forcing the transformation are economic conditions, eroding public confidence, accountability demands, and demographic shifts resulting in increased numbers of people from historically underrepresented groups going to college. More people are participating in higher education than ever before, yet the resources supporting the enterprise are not keeping pace with the demand. Because of these and other factors, legislators, parents, governing boards, and students want colleges and universities to reemphasize student learning and personal development as the primary goals of undergraduate education. In short, people want to know that higher education is preparing students to lead productive lives after college, including the ability to deal effectively with such major societal challenges as poverty, illiteracy, crime, and environmental exploitation. (ACPA, 1996, p. 1)

An early publication in student affairs, *Pieces of Eight* (Appleton et al., 1978), chronicles the growth and early development of the field. In the book, the authors argue that student affairs was organized from the bottom up. In a particularly unflattering pronouncement, these early historians of the student affairs field stated, "We began by serving needs that had been pushed to the periphery, and some would argue that the field has remained there ever since" (p. 12). The argument advanced is that a void was created when faculty assumed the research role of the German research institutions. Someone other than faculty had to fill the role of caretakers and disciplinarians in the residence halls, dining halls, and out-of-classroom venues. In the years that have transpired since the writing of *Pieces of Eight*, a wider perspective on the purposes and underlying assumptions of the student affairs field has emerged. Despite the persistence of the argument that student affairs was "founded by default," others have argued that the field emerged as a result of a strongly defined need (Manning, 1996).

Regardless of where one falls on the continuum of opinions about the founding of the field, it is hard to deny that student affairs has stood the test of time. Despite any arguments to the contrary (which often emerge during budget cuts), student affairs divisions and the services, programs, and policies they administer and provide are firmly entrenched in higher education institutions. Although there are ranges of approaches to the provision of student affairs programs and services (e.g., directive, student initiated, high quality, catch as catch can), student affairs exists in some shape or form on every U.S. college campus. While the current state of student affairs is ensured, the question of the future is less certain. How will the student affairs field meet the needs of students, play a part in fulfilling the goals of the institution, and work to create an environment where learning opportunities lead to high-quality education and, ultimately, engaged and successful students?

Student Affairs Philosophy, Administrative
Structures, and Student Engagement

In this book we argue that the founding documents of the student affairs field (ACE, 1937, 1949) provide a firm foundation upon which to build current student affairs practice (see chapter 1). The whole student philosophy persists as a worthy foundation upon which to build individual and institutional student affairs practice. But this philosophy cannot be considered in isolation, neither out of context from the institution in which that philosophy is practiced, nor out of context with the current climate of the U.S. higher education system as a whole. This is particularly the case in the current and continuing higher education climate of high tuition, competition, and lack of public confidence about higher education's value.

The context in which student affairs exists creates both opportunity and constraint. In such an environment, flexibility in theory and practice must by necessity be a major characteristic of the student affairs field. Student affairs exists in a context rich with diverse stakeholders, extensive choice of administrative practices, and a constantly changing student body. While jokes often are made that it is easier to move a graveyard than to change higher education, student affairs cannot be counted among those adverse to change. Perhaps because we work so closely with young people or because obsolete ideas can have life-altering repercussions, student affairs is an area of higher education administration that adjusts to and even embraces change. In fact, those who are uncomfortable with ambiguity and change are often advised to choose another life's work.

Loci of Change in Student Affairs

There are several loci of change to which student affairs educators must attend: the national system, profession, and institution. In addition to being informed about the levels and influences of these different levels of influence, student affairs educators reflect on their practice to make the appropriately professional and developmental choices. Without this flexibility and malleability, student affairs educators risk becoming obsolete, a condition that the competitive and budget-driven state of higher education will not accommodate. The models of student affairs practice outlined in this book must be similarly able to accommodate systemwide, professionwide, and institutional adaptations.

National Systemwide Change

A favorite activity of observers of higher education is to document changes and trends in the field. The following sections summarize information from recent documents outlining trends in the field and apply this understanding to the models proposed in this book.

Critical Issues in Higher Education and Student Affairs

An underlying assumption of student affairs practice is that the context of national higher education is dynamic and ever changing. The pace of education has escalated and promises to stay at or increase in speed and intensity. Some have characterized this state as "permanent white water." The national systemwide trends and developments outlined below (i.e., technology, evolution of faculty roles, and internationalization) are a sample of issues to be considered in the context of the stimulating environment in which student affairs educators work. In the context of the models discussed in this book, professionwide changes discussed here include a shift from teaching to learning, advancing social justice, and encouraging sustainability. Institution-level trends related to the models include fit with institutional mission and culture.

Technology and the Nature of Higher Education Institutions

Levine (2000) predicted that three basic types of institutions will dominate U.S. higher education in the future: "'brick universities,' or traditional residential institutions; 'click universities,' or new, usually commercial virtual universities . . .; and 'brick and click' universities, a combination of the first two" (p. B10). He argues that, regardless of the conveniences that online classes, programs, and services offer, students "also want a physical space where they can interact with others and obtain expert advice and assistance face-to-face" (p. B10). Although some may argue with Levine's conclusions about the prevalence of different kinds of institutions, the task at hand in this chapter is to consider the models discussed in this book in light of these three types of institutions.

Technology, student affairs, and learning. Whether one works in a traditional "brick university," a "click," or a "brick and click university," technology has had a major influence on student affairs practice. The World Wide Web and the sites it supports are a ubiquitous part of university life. In a short period of time, technology has become a major force in our lives and professions. Many services, programs, and policies of student affairs currently are available on institutional home pages or will be shortly. The majority of students, faculty, and staff members have a high degree of access to technology and proficiency with its use. As a method of communication (e.g., e-mail, text messaging), means of service and program delivery (e.g., websites), and medium for administration (e.g., databases, attachments), technology hopefully provides a more efficient way to meet student affairs goals.

The challenge for institutions that engage either traditional or innovative models of student affairs practice will be to use technology in ways that encourage critical thinking, build ways to apply knowledge to problem solving, and help students expand their concepts of identity and interaction with others (ACPA, 1996). The use of computer technology provides student affairs with the same challenge as any other technology (e.g., telephone, paper, administrative procedures), how to use it toward the goal of student learning and success.

Evolution of Faculty Roles

Another trend identified by Levine (2000) is the growing independence of faculty from specific institutions. According to his projections, selected faculty will become more star-like, command high salaries, and grow to be increasingly disconnected from specific college communities. Rather than a traditional, institutionally based model, faculty scholarship and intellectual endeavors will be pursued through independent, noninstitutional means. Again, whether or not one agrees with Levine's projections, this trend points to a distinct role for student affairs professionals. A change in faculty roles certainly will precipitate a change in student affairs roles as a shift in one part of the organization results in a simultaneous shift in other parts (Allen & Cherrey, 2000).

The DEEP study found a connection between faculty roles, students, and engagement (see chapter 2). The researchers who studied the 20 DEEP institutions found that engaged students existed in a context of engaged faculty and vice versa. Although one can proffer the chicken and egg argument about whether engaged faculty precede engaged students or vice versa, the influence of mutual engagement on these two populations cannot be overstated. Higher education scholars who project trends about faculty often miss their close link with students. While student affairs folklore often speaks to a disconnection between faculty and students, the DEEP research found this separation to be overstated. When students are engaged in the academic and social aspects of campus, the environment is rich with opportunities for learning.

Levine's (2000) projection about independent faculty calls even more attention to the need, expressed in this book, for academic and student affairs to be more closely connected. An absence of territoriality between student and academic affairs and an "unshakeable focus on student learning" at DEEP institutions create conditions for success in student engagement and graduation. Although the nature of student affairs professionals' relationship with faculty may shift, the importance of a continued, ongoing, and deepening relationship remains.

Globalization of Higher Education

Another nationally oriented change within higher education is the globalization of U.S. higher education. World economies and social systems are no longer isolated but part of a global context. What occurs in one country (e.g., the events of September 11, 2001) strongly influences the higher education climate in other countries (e.g., increased attendance due to curtailed foreign exchange to the United States). Among other countries, China, India, and the European Union (EU) are developing their higher education systems for economic and social gains. These countries are consciously and actively competing with the United States for students. China is aggressively expanding its higher education system to accommodate increased economic growth and entry into the world economy. "India is increasing its educational marketing and gaining students all the time" (Society for College and University Planning, 2004, p. 3). The EU, through the Bologna Declaration (European Ministers of Education, 1999), is undergoing "massification." EU higher education institutions are expanding access, opening admission systems, and changing centuries of limited access to higher education. Through the Bologna Declaration, EU countries are standardizing curricula, credit requirements, and the number of years necessary for degree attainment. Such standardization across the entire EU promises to create a higher education system unparalleled even within the rich histories of the EU countries. These developments, coupled with the global shrinking technological activities discussed above, promise to significantly alter the face of U.S. higher education over the next 10 years. Already, the discussion about the diminishing dominance of U.S. higher education has begun.

The globalization occurring within higher education systems is reflected in student affairs practice. Whichever model is selected for use on a campus, it must have far enough reach to encompass the scope of this globalization. In particular, rich student learning experiences that encourage global citizenship, critical thinking, and an understanding of issues larger than the immediate self play an essential part in the goal of internationalization and globalization. The old workhorse programs of study abroad, short-term study tours, and on-campus internationalization certainly strive to meet these goals. Newer programs of community and service learning and programs that ask students to reflect on their cultural, social, and political place in the world (Freire, 1990) also further these goals.

Professionwide Change

In the context of the national changes discussed above, the student affairs profession has undergone significant growth and change.

Shift from Teaching to Learning

Through the foresight of student affairs leaders and scholars, a shift from teaching to learning was projected and thoroughly discussed in *The Student Learning Imperative* (ACPA, 1996), *Powerful Partnerships* (AAHE et al., 1998), and *Principles of Good Practice for Student Affairs* (ACPA & NASPA, 1997). Throughout these documents, the authors reinforce that "focusing on learning rather than instruction is a fundamental shift in perspective" (p. 1). These documents also advocate the position that a shift to learning must occur in the context of increased diversity on college campuses. This diversity comes in the shape of types of institutions, student characteristics, and range of learning opportunities, among others.

In the face of the growing pressures on higher education, Levine (2000) is alarmed about an eroding commonality of purpose within the college experience. He provocatively asks the question, "how can they [institutions of higher education] create communities that are sufficiently vital to attract and retain faculty members?" (p. B10). Those of us in student affairs can easily imagine an answer such that student affairs educators create the bridge between rich in- and out-of-class-room learning experiences. In particular, student affairs exerts a major influence when creating engaged communities. Our emphasis on community building, social justice, and holistic education puts our field in a unique position to be a consistent influence in building a common experience throughout the college years. Clearly, Levine's challenge of creating vital communities is one student affairs can embrace as part of its legacy of community involvement. These efforts can create a rich student learning environment for students.

Advancing Social Justice

Regardless of the student affairs model, student affairs educators have long taken the lead in promoting diversity, multicultural perspectives, and social justice. As stated in *The Student Learning Imperative* (ACPA, 1996), "*Good practice in student affairs builds supportive and inclusive communities.* Student learning occurs best in communities that value diversity, promote social responsibility, encourage discussion and debate, recognize accomplishments, and foster a sense of belonging among their members" (p. 4). The student affairs discussion about diversity has evolved throughout the years from the "counting" perspective of cultural diversity to a richer perspective of social justice and pluralism (Hurtado, Milem, Clayton-Pedersen, & Allen, 1999; Pope, Reynolds, & Mueller, 2004). The campus effort to promote social justice for gay, lesbian, bisexual, and transsexual students is one of many student affairs efforts aimed to fundamentally transform the campus to a more socially just context.

The next step for student affairs concerning social justice is to more meaningfully engage the entire campus in the pluralism efforts they have initiated. Although efforts to promote tolerance in the residence halls, extend campus organization privileges to a range of affinity groups, and increase services for students with identities not previously acknowledged on campus have substantially increased through the efforts of student affairs, these achievements have not gained their full effect on the larger organizational culture. In the context of institutionwide influence, several DEEP institutions have opened their doors wide to provide education, leadership opportunities, and career potential to a substantial diversity of students. These institutions have broken the traditional mold of teaching, research, and service to create a vision of higher education apt for the 21st century. For some of these institutions, increasing access in the face of the growing diversity of U.S. higher education students has social justice roots. To others, expansion of the range of students welcomed into an institution is necessary for survival. Shifting demographics warrant opening the doors of higher education wider if institutions are to sustain or expand their student populations.

The innovative models of student affairs practice advanced in this book hold substantial potential for obtaining institutionwide support for diversity efforts. Each model, in its own way, speaks to the need for greater cooperation and respect between academic and student affairs. With a professional and learning-based stance, the educational issues advanced by both academic and student affairs can be mutually reinforced. In the absence of competition, faculty and administrators can work toward similar goals—whether those goals are social justice or an issue related to the institutional mission. Notably, the longstanding debate about the relative importance of academic versus student affairs was absent, perhaps not deemed as important, at the DEEP schools. All were engaged in student learning.

Encouraging Sustainability

"The choice for student affairs is simple: We can pursue a course that engages us in the central mission of our institutions or retreat to the margins in the hope that we will avoid the inconvenience of change" (ACPA, 1996, p. 1). In the market-driven climate of U.S. higher education, the concept of sustainability has several meanings. One meaning entails the resources needed to successfully offer programs and services, shape environments, and craft policy. This concern undoubtedly shapes much of the activity involved in increasing financial resources through auxiliary activities and fee-funded departments and activities.

But sustainability extends beyond financial stability and viability. Similar to Levine's question about faculty viability discussed above, student affairs educators must similarly ask, "How can a student affairs division be crafted in such a way that high-quality staff are recruited and retained within the institution? How can student affairs educators be professionally motivated and developed through the course of their life-long career? How can the human resources of the profession be nurtured within the context of a healthy student affairs field?" Therefore, sustainability from this perspective involves human as well as capital resources. The overall health of the student affairs field in the context of a healthy and robust global higher education environment must be considered.

Similar to the DEEP finding that engaged faculty lead to engaged students and vice versa, engaged student affairs educators take up the same dynamic. This book has emphasized the topics of engagement and learning. What would happen if the models of student affairs practice embraced on campus had the same singular focus on learning that the DEEP institutions possessed? What would professional development look like with a learning focus? How can student affairs use the models proposed in this book to infuse an intellectually charged theory-to-practice-to-theory approach?

Institution-Specific Change

Finally, all student affairs offices and divisions exist within individual colleges and universities. The nature of these specific institutions will most certainly shape the changes occurring on a micro- and macrolevel.

Matching Models to Institutional Goals and Cultures

The DEEP research uncovered a condition for engagement rooted in the heart of higher education.

DEEP schools have one characteristic in common: their mission is 'alive.' Faculty members, administrators, staff, students, and others use it to explain their behavior and to talk about what the institution is, the direction it is heading, and how their work contributes to its goals. (Kuh et al., 2005, p. 27)

The mission of the institution and the division of student affairs, regardless of model employed, is integrally linked to the means the institution uses to foster student engagement and success. At DEEP schools, the link between mission and practice is neither accidental nor haphazard. We cannot overemphasize the importance of congruence between student affairs and institutional mission, purpose, and goals. This congruence and integration is particularly relevant in the context of the two institutional goals explored in the DEEP study: high student engagement and student success as measured by high graduation rates. Student affairs divisions are deeply implicated in both goals.

Any choice of student affairs models discussed in this book must take the individual institutional context and culture into account. Kuh and Whitt (1988) define culture as "normative and social glue . . . based on shared values and beliefs" (p. 10). Culture, in their discussion, serves four purposes: it (a) conveys a sense of identity, (b) facilitates commitment to an entity, (c) enhances the stability of a group's social system, and (d) serves as a sense-making device that guides and shapes behavior. They describe several potent campus cultures. Faculty culture, valuing autonomy and collegiality, focuses on the "pursuit and dissemination of knowledge as the purpose of higher education" (p. 76). The student subculture involves "taken for granted patterns" (van Maanen, 1987, p. 5 as quoted in Kuh & Whitt, 1988, p. 84) and, similar to faculty, can act as a conservative force. In other words, certain aspects of faculty and student cultures can maintain the culture as it exists and discourage change. These and other cultures on campus require the student affairs educator to be aware of the context in which they perform their practice. In complex cultural organizations such as colleges and universities, the choice of which student affairs model to employ does not entail a single, static decision. Rather, this choice must be made in the context of a dynamic, ever-changing cultural environment.

Jablonski (personal communication, 2005) discussed the confluence of various, sometimes conflicting cultures on campuses where she has practiced student affairs. These include the student, administrative, faculty, and, notably for her context, athletic cultures. Rather than thinking of campus culture as a monolithically defined entity with a singular response from the division of student affairs, the approach on this type of campus must be flexible enough to match the numerous campus cultures as they are encountered. An approach that works with students may fail miserably with faculty or administrators. Obviously, a response geared for student leaders may not work with athletes who have a different status and set of privileges on a National Collegiate Athletic Association Division I campus. Each rich subculture (e.g., parent, legislative) has its own set of defining characteristics. In a multifaceted manner, student affairs educators must blend and negotiate their practice with the overall institutional mission and individual campus subcultures. Therefore, mission and campus cultures (literally considered in the plural) must be understood when one determines the student affairs model that best meets the needs of the institution.

Transforming From a Traditional to Innovative Model

The discussion about the models presented in this book certainly raises the question, "How can I change the current traditional model of student affairs practice to an innovative model that focuses on student learning?" The DEEP project provides lessons concerning ways in which a campus can make the shift to innovative student affairs practice.

Leadership. It may sound like an old saw, but leadership is key to creating rich student learning-centered environments. At several DEEP institutions, new presidents or provosts (whether hired from within or outside the institution) served as catalysts for change. The new leaders infused ideas about interdisciplinary and collaborative student learning and cooperative approaches to university administration. They urged a renewed commitment to student learning; they made resources available and changed the climate. In essence, the DEEP research indicated that leadership, particularly at the executive level, indeed makes a difference. These leaders set the tone for what to emphasize. They role modeled collaboration and respectful interaction. They inspired, urged, cajoled, and required. They took their role as educators seriously and saw themselves, regardless of style, as responsible for leading the effort concerning student learning.

Similar to the presidents and provosts observed at the DEEP institutions, a new VPSA could certainly provide leadership and an infusion of enthusiasm for new models of practice. Many student affairs leaders use their "honeymoon" period to push controversial ideas and changes. Although other catalysts effect change as well, new leadership is a formidable option.

Institutional Crisis. Crisis was often a catalyst that created a shift to more innovative models of student affairs practice. At times, the crisis was budget or enrollment driven. More likely, the catalyst was a moment in time when the institution faced a reality not previously envisioned. At one DEEP institution, a failed grant proposal provided feedback that the institution was not "anything special." This pointed and upsetting assessment forced administrators and faculty to examine their mission and their approach to teaching and student affairs practice. With a renewed commitment to interdisciplinary and learning-centered approaches, a second grant request was successful. College members point to this pivotal moment as the catalyst for renewed commitment to student learning. The new perspective inevitably led to changes in how student affairs was organized.

Technology. Whether through library-based learning opportunities, web-based approaches to institutional communication, or technology-assisted programs and service provisions, many DEEP institutions use technology to advance student learning. The introduction of technology as a different way to practice pushes a re-examination of the ways that student affairs divisions are organized. Established ways of communicating are bound to change with the introduction of the immediacy of the Internet. With students asking for more and more services to be web- and technology-based, student affairs divisions are hard pressed to continue to use models based on pre-web practices.

Winston Salem State University was the most striking example of change due to technology. The decision was made that policies, procedures, and campus communication would be delivered solely through the web. The effect on the physical appearance of the campus was striking. The environment was free of the clutter and profusion of flyers, posters, and notices that generally fill a campus. But, more important, the effect on the sense of community and informed nature of the students was formidable. Students knew how to negotiate the campus bureaucracy. They knew where to get the information they needed to complete their work as students. The web served as a infrastructure to organize the community. Few places have achieved this level of infrastructure-community symbiosis. One can imagine the ways in which this approach shapes both the learning environment and student affairs practice.

Professional Development. Another way that student affairs divisions can shift their approach from traditional to innovative is by remaining current with the developments in the field. The authors of this book reviewed the influence of pivotal documents and think pieces. One can trace the development of thinking about student affairs practice through these documents. *The Student Personnel Point of View, 1937* (ACE, 1937), *The Student Learning Imperative* (ACPA, 1996), *Powerful Partnerships* (AAHE et al., 1998), and *Learning Reconsidered* (ACPA & NASPA, 2004), among others, can provide a philosophical foundation upon which to base student affairs practice. With each philosophical rendition, thinking about student affairs practice is refined and enriched. By remaining aware of these developments within the field, campus leaders can transform their model of practice to incorporate the new ideas and, therefore, enrich student learning within their division and across the campus.

These are only a few of the catalysts that can serve to urge a move from the traditional to innovative models of student affairs practice. While the goal of student learning is universal to U.S. higher education, the achievement of that goal is a campus-by-campus decision. As such, the unique historical confluences and mission imperatives that drive any change in practice must also be achieved on a case-by-case basis.

Some Thoughts About Student Affairs Graduate Preparation

Similar to administrators on campus, graduate preparation faculty fit their educational efforts into national, profession, and institutional contexts. As we consider these contexts, a question quickly emerges: Does graduate preparation as it is currently conceived prepare students to negotiate the diverse, dynamic practices of the innovative models presented here? To encourage a shift in thinking from the traditional to innovative models of student affairs practice, perhaps the following traditional beliefs prevent graduate students from pursuing a learning situation that reflects the full dynamism of the field.

1. Student affairs is generally the same across different institutions.
2. The student affairs lessons from 30 years ago still guide the field.
3. The model of student affairs practice experienced in graduate school is readily transferable to the new professional's first job.
4. The teaching role of student affairs is paramount.

Instead of these beliefs, a newer set of innovative beliefs is suggested:

1. The complexity of higher education warrants a diversity of perspectives concerning student affairs practice.
2. Student affairs is about learning in all situations and contexts.
3. The goals of student and academic affairs have significant overlap.
4. Student success and high levels of engagement warrant a flexible, mission-centric, and context-specific approach to student affairs practice.

Student affairs graduate preparation has a substantial influence on the overall culture of the field. Its central role warrants careful consideration about the complexity of thinking encouraged among the future generations of student affairs practitioners. Does graduate education adequately reflect the current thinking about learning? Do graduate preparation programs engender the flexibility necessary for the innovative student models? Several DEEP researchers who are graduate-preparation faculty asked themselves, "Does graduate preparation as it is currently conceived prepare students for the engagement and student success rich environments reflected in the DEEP institutions?" Perhaps it is time for the field to conceptually catch up to the place where practice has led us.

Conclusion

Student affairs has a major role to play in creating the conditions for student engagement and success. In 1985, Garland wrote a monograph called, *Serving More than Students*, in which he proposed a new role for student affairs educators: integrator. More than 20 years ago, he suggested that student affairs educators were in a unique position to bridge the gap between student and academic affairs. The DEEP researchers expounded on this integrator role, expressed in a collaborative, noncompetitive style between student and academic affairs, leading to student engagement and success (Kuh et al., 2005). By deliberating choosing the model of student affairs that advances the campus mission and fits the campus cultures, the integrator role envisioned by Garland could be achieved.

Appendix: Research Method

This appendix briefly summarizes the research methods used in the Documenting Effective Educational Practices (DEEP) project, a two-year study carried out under the auspices of the National Survey of Student Engagement (NSSE) Institute for Effective Educational Practice at the Indiana University Center for Postsecondary Research. A more complete explanation of the research methodology is Kuh et al. (2005).

Introduction

The purpose of the DEEP project was to develop a comprehensive understanding of what 20 high-performing institutions do to promote student engagement and success. A research team was assembled and used qualitative case study design (Merriam, 2002) to discover and document the policies, programs and practices, and conditions associated with higher than predicted student engagement and success.

Research Team

The DEEP research team consisted of 24 people intentionally chosen for their different areas of expertise and background. Some were primarily scholars; others were current or former academic and student affairs practitioners. The team was large enough to allow two multiple-day site visits to each school (for a total of 40 visits) between fall 2002 and winter 2004.

DEEP team members met for three days in August 2002 to review the research process, discuss site visit procedures and logistics, and develop data collection protocols. The team met four times during the data collection phase by conference call or face-to-face meetings. Site visit teams communicated regularly via e-mail and telephone before, during, and following site visits to discuss data analysis procedures and interpretations, make decisions about various aspects of the work, and conduct data analysis.

Sample

An ideal-typical case selection process was used, whereby the researchers identified institutions representing "models" or desirable examples of colleges and universities with demonstrable track records for promoting student success (LeCompte & Preissle, 1993). Sample institutions were drawn from a potential pool of 700 four-year colleges and universities that participated in the NSSE between 2000 and 2002. The initial pool of 700 was narrowed down to institutions that had higher-than-predicted student engagement results and higher-than-predicted six-year graduation rates. Regression models calculated the predicted student engagement scores and graduation rates. The number of institutions that met these two criteria exceeded the target of 20 schools, which was the maximum number the project resources (e.g., financial, personnel, time) could accommodate. At this point additional criteria were considered: institutional size, type (e.g., 4-year institution), control (e.g., public or private), and geographic locale (region, rural/urban).

Data Collection

Teams of three to five researchers visited each of the 20 DEEP schools for the first site visit. Prior to the site visit, an on-campus DEEP site visit coordinator was identified to facilitate the research, gather documents for team review, and schedule interviews and focus groups. In advance, the site visit team reviewed written or web-based documents, such as institutional histories, catalogs, admissions materials, policy statements, student handbooks, organizational charts, student newspapers and other campus publications or videos, accreditation reports, and institutional self-studies. Reviewing campus websites alerted the visiting team to current issues and events. NSSE survey data for the visiting institution were also reviewed for possible lines of inquiry and exploration.

On site, the research team obtained data through interviews, focus groups, observation, and document analysis about the programs, policies, and practices that contributed to student success. The five NSSE clusters of effective educational practice (i.e., level of academic challenge, active and collaborative learning, student-faculty interactions, enriching educational experiences, and supportive campus environment) were a conceptual map to guide data collection and analysis. The teams also sought to discover programs, policies, and practices that were not encompassed by the NSSE framework but that respondents identified as related to student engagement and success. Peer debriefing among site visit team members occurred on site to test assumptions and determine themes and interpretations. A final meeting was held with key informants (e.g., provost, site coordinator) for feedback and verification purposes.

Following the initial site visit, site team members drafted an "interim report," which described the college or university context; featured relevant policies, programs, and practices; and identified factors and conditions that respondents and other data sources suggested were related to student engagement and success. The interim report summarized tentative themes warranting additional consideration and identified unanswered questions and topics for exploration during the second visit. The interim report was sent to the campus site visit coordinator with the request that it be distributed widely on campus for member checking.

Second site visit teams were usually composed of two or three people, at least one of whom was a member of the first site visit group and one of whom was new to the campus. This approach ensured both continuity and "fresh eyes." During the second visit, debriefing meetings were held with groups of faculty, students, staff, and others. The interim report was discussed in an effort to correct errors and identify practices needing further attention. Snowball sampling was used to identify additional respondents from whom site team members could learn different or potentially instructive views. Following the second visit, a final report was produced and sent to the institution with a request for additional member checking, feedback, and commentary. This document became the primary data source for analysis. Both the interim and final site visit reports include descriptive and interpretative material so that readers can make explicit connections between the goals of the study, the findings, and emerging themes (Merriam, 1998).

In all, team members interacted individually or in groups with more than 2,500 people (1,233 students, 750 faculty members, and 526 others, including student affairs professionals, librarians, and instructional technology staff). Some people were interviewed more than once. Team members sat in on approximately 60 classes, attended more than 30 campus events, dined in about 20 campus locations, rode buses, participated in campus tours, walked on campus, and visited student centers.

Data Analysis

Analyzing qualitative data from multiple sites is an iterative process (Coffey & Atkinson, 1996). In this study, data collection and analysis became more systematic with each site visit. This iterative, emergent design allowed team members to continually improve the amount and quality of the information gathered. Through a hermeneutic and dialectic process (Guba & Lincoln, 1989), different interpretations, claims, concerns, and issues were shared, understood, considered, critiqued, and acted upon. The objective was to elicit ongoing interpretive impressions from research team members and institutional stakeholders—honoring and simultaneously testing their constructions and interpretations of tentative claims against the collected data. Intra- and intersite data analysis was conducted. To analyze the data in the richest way possible, different combinations of research team members met during data collection and analysis when circumstances allowed (e.g., professional meetings, conference calls).

During the data analysis phase, voluntary team members identified key data elements from the reports. These elements were the smallest units (e.g., phrases, sentences, paragraphs) that stood alone and revealed meaningful information (Lincoln & Guba, 1985). To manage the process, NUD*IST/NVivo software (Richards, 2002) was employed. NUD*IST required the NSSE staff and select research teams members to read data line by line, considering the meaning of each word, sentence, and idea (Creswell, 1998).

Trustworthiness

Triangulation, peer debriefing, member checking, and searching for disconfirming evidence to establish credibility were employed to establish trustworthiness (Creswell & Miller, 2000; Lincoln & Guba, 1985). Preliminary hypotheses, assumptions, and interpretations were challenged through peer debriefings during site visits and afterward via e-mail and conference calls. Interim and final reports were distributed to the entire research team to inform their data gathering at subsequent site visits. Interim and final reports were shared with respondents to confirm or challenge their accuracy and credibility. NSSE Institute staff reviewed every interim report to scrutinize data and preliminary interpretations.

To provide evidence that the inquiry decisions were logical and defensible, an audit trail was established (Lincoln & Guba, 1985; Whitt & Kuh, 1991). This trail included raw data (e.g., tapes, interview notes, and documents), field notes, and interview and document summary forms. Case analysis forms (e.g., multiple drafts of site visit reports), evidence of member checking, and materials relating to research team intentions, including notes of debriefings and staff meeting minutes and correspondence, also became part of this trail.

References

Allen, K., & Cherrey, C. (2000). *Systemic leadership: Enriching the meaning of our work*. Lanham, MD: University Press of America.

Alpert, D. (1986). Performance and paralysis: The organizational context of the American research university. *Journal of Higher Education, 56*(3), 1–19.

Ambler, D. (2000). Organizational and administrative models. In M. J. Barr, M. J. Desler, & Associates, *The handbook of student affairs administration* (pp. 121–133). San Francisco: Jossey-Bass.

American Association for Higher Education, American College Personnel Association, & National Association of Student Personnel Administrators. (1998). *Powerful partnerships: A shared responsibility for learning*. Washington, DC: American College Personnel Association.

American College Personnel Association. (1996). *The student learning imperative*. Washington, DC: Author.

American College Personnel Association & National Association of Student Personnel Administrators. (1999). *Principles of good practice for student affairs*. Washington, DC: Author.

American College Personnel Association & National Association of Student Personnel Administrators. (2004). *Learning reconsidered: A campus-wide focus on the student experience*. Washington, DC: Author.

American Council on Education. (1937). *The student personnel point of view*. Washington, DC: Author.

American Council on Education. (1949). *The student personnel point of view*. Washington, DC: Author.

Appleton, J. R., Briggs, C. M., & Rhatigan, J. J. (1978). *Pieces of eight: The rites, roles, and styles of the dean by eight who have been there.* Portland, OR: NASPA.

Association of College and University Housing Officers-International Residential College Task Force. (1996, April). The residential nexus: A focus on student learning. *Talking Stick: Bringing Academics to the Residence Halls, 13*(7), 6–10.

Astin, A. W. (1977). *Four critical years.* San Francisco: Jossey-Bass.

Astin, A. W. (1984). Student involvement: A developmental theory for higher education. *Journal of College Student Personnel, 25,* 297–308.

Astin, A. W. (1985). *Achieving educational excellence.* San Francisco: Jossey-Bass.

Astin, A. W. (1991). *Assessment for excellence: The philosophy and practice of assessment and evaluation in higher education.* American Council on Education Series on Higher Education. Washington, DC/New York: American Council on Education and Macmillan.

Astin, A. W. (1993). *What matters in college? Four critical years revisited.* San Francisco: Jossey-Bass.

Baldridge, J. V., Curtis, D. V., Ecker, G., & Riley, G. L. (1980). *Policy making and effective leadership.* San Francisco: Jossey-Bass.

Ballard, S., & Long, P. N. (2004, November–December). Profiles in partnership: Finding strength in collaborative leadership. *About Campus, 9*(5), 16–22.

Ballou, R. A. (1997, November–December). Reorganizing student affairs for the twenty-first century. *About Campus, 2*(5), 24–25.

Bandura, A. (2001). Social cognitive theory: An agentic perspective. *Annual Review of Psychology, 52,* 1–26.

Banning, J. (1978). *Campus ecology: A perspective for student affairs.* Cincinnati, OH: NASPA Monograph.

Barr, M. J. (2000). The importance of institutional mission. In M. J. Barr, M. K. Desler, & Associates, *The handbook of student affairs administration* (2nd ed., pp. 25–36). San Francisco: Jossey-Bass.

Barr, R., & Tagg, J. T. (1995, November/December). From teaching to learning: A new paradigm for undergraduate education. *Change, 27,* 12–25.

Benedict, A., Casper, B., Larson, L., Littlepage, G., & Panke, J. (2000). Utilizing paraprofessionals to expand student outreach. National Career Development Association annual conference, Pittsburgh, PA.

Birnbaum, R. (1991). *How colleges work.* San Francisco: Jossey-Bass.

Blau, P. M. (1970). A formal theory of differentiation in organizations. *American Sociological Review, 35,* 201–218.

Blau, P. M. (1970/1973). *The organization of academic work.* New York: John Wiley & Sons.

Blau, P. M. (1972). Interdependence and hierarchy in organizations. *Social Science Research, 1*(1), 1–24.

Blimling, G. S., Whitt, E. J., & Associates. (1999). *Good practice in student affairs: Principles to foster student learning.* San Francisco: Jossey-Bass.

Bloland, P. A., Stamatakos, L. C., & Rogers, R. R. (1994). *Reform in student affairs: A critique of student development.* Greensboro, NC: ERIC Counseling and Student Services Clearinghouse.

Bolman, L. G., & Deal, T. E. (2003). *Reframing organizations: Artistry, choice, and leadership* (3rd ed.). San Francisco: Jossey-Bass.

Bourassa, D. & Kruger, K. (2001). The national dialogue on academic and student affairs collaboration. *New Directions for Higher Education, 16,* 9–38.

Bowen, H. R. (1977). *Investment in learning: The individual and social value of American higher education.* San Francisco: Jossey-Bass.

Boyer, E. L. (1987). *College: The undergraduate experience in America.* New York: Harper & Row.

Boyer, E. L. (1990). *Scholarship reconsidered: Priorities of the professoriate.* San Francisco: Jossey-Bass.

Breen, D. G. (1970). *Survey of selected programs for student leadership training at colleges and universities.* (Eric Document Reproduction Service No. 044073). DeKalb: Northern Illinois University.

Brown, R. D. (1972). *Student development in tomorrow's higher education: A return to the academy.* (Student Personnel Series No. 16). Washington, DC: ACPA.

Bruffee, K. A. (1993). *Collaborative learning: Higher education, interdependence, and the authority of knowledge.* Baltimore, MD: Johns Hopkins University Press.

Burke, J. C. (2004). The many faces of accountability. In J. C. Burke & Associates, *Achieving accountability in higher education* (pp. 1–24). San Francisco: Jossey-Bass.

Cage, M. C. (1992, November 18). To shield academic programs from cuts, many colleges pare student services. *The Chronicle of Higher Education,* p. A25.

Caple, R. B. (1996). The learning debate: A historical perspective. *Journal of College Student Development, 37*(2), 193–202.

Caple, R. B. (1998). *To mark the beginning: A social history of college student affairs.* Lanham, MD: University Press of America.

Carey, K. (2004). *A matter of degrees: Improving graduation rates in four-year colleges and universities.* Washington, DC: Education Trust.

Chandler, E. M. (1973/1986). Student affairs administration in transition. In G. L. Saddlemire & A. L. Rentz (Eds.), *Student affairs: A profession's heritage* (pp. 334–345). Alexandria, VA: ACPA.

Chickering, A. W. (1969). *Education and identity.* San Francisco: Jossey-Bass.

Chickering, A. W., & Gamson, Z. F. (1987). Seven principles for good practice in undergraduate education. *AAHE Bulletin, 39*(7), 3–7.

Chickering, A. W., & Reisser, L. (1993). *Education and identity* (2nd ed.). San Francisco: Jossey-Bass.

Chronicle 1999–2000 Almanac. *The Chronicle of Higher Education.* Retrieved July 8, 2005, from http://chronicle.com/prm/weekly/1999/facts/14stu.htm.

Chronicle Almanac 2004–5. *The Chronicle of Higher Education.* Retrieved July 8, 2005, from http://chronicle.com/prm/weekly/almanac/2004/nation/0101602.htm.

Clothier, R. C. (1931/1986). College personnel principles and functions. In G. Saddlemire & A. Rentz (Eds.), *Student affairs: A profession's heritage* (pp. 9–20). Alexandria, VA: American College Personnel Association.

Coffey, A., & Atkinson, P. (1996). *Making sense of qualitative data: Complementary research strategies.* Thousand Oaks, CA: Sage.

Cohen, M. D., & March, J. G. (1986). *Leadership and ambiguity: The American college presidency* (2nd ed.). Boston: Harvard Business School Press.

Crane, W. J. (1963/1983). Curb service administration. In B. A. Belson & L. E. Fitzgerald (Eds.), *Thus, we spoke. ACPA—NAWDAC 1958–1975* (pp. 107–118). Carbondale, IL: ACPA.

Creswell, J. W. (1998). *Qualitative inquiry and research design: Choosing among five traditions.* Thousand Oaks, CA: Sage.

Creswell, J. W., & Miller, D. L. (2000). Determining validity in qualitative inquiry. *Theory into Practice, 39*(3), 124–130.

Delworth, U., & Hanson, G. (1980). *Student services: A handbook for the profession.* San Francisco: Jossey-Bass.

Delworth, U., & Hanson, G. (1989). *Student services: A handbook for the profession* (2nd ed.). San Francisco: Jossey-Bass.

Dewey, J. (1916). *Democracy and education.* New York: Macmillan.

Dewey, J. (1940). *Education today.* New York: G. P. Putnam's Sons.

Doyle, J. (2004). Student affairs division's integration of student learning principles. *NASPA Journal, 41,* 375–394.

Dungy, G. J. (2003). Organization and functions of student affairs. In S. R. Komives, D. B. Woodard, Jr., & Associates, *Student services: A handbook for the profession* (4th ed., pp. 339–357). San Francisco: Jossey-Bass.

Education Commission of the States. (1995). *Making Quality Count in Undergraduate Education*. Denver, CO: Education Commission of the States.

Engstrom, C. M., & Tinto, V. (2000). Developing partnerships with academic affairs to enhance student learning. In M. J. Barr, M. K. Desler, & Associates, *The handbook of student affairs administration* (2nd ed., pp. 425–452). San Francisco: Jossey-Bass.

European Ministers of Education. (1999). *The European higher education area*. Bologna, Italy: Unpublished paper.

Evans, N. J., & Reason, R. D. (2001). Guiding principles: A review and analysis of student affairs philosophical statements. *Journal of College Student Development, 42*, 359–377.

Fenske, R. (1989). Evolution of the student services profession. In U. Delworth, G. R. Hanson, & Associates, *Student services: A handbook for the profession* (2nd ed., pp. 25–56). San Francisco: Jossey-Bass.

Freire, P. (1985). *The politics of education: Culture, power and liberation*. Hadley, MA: Bergin & Garvey.

Freire, P. (1990). *Pedagogy of the oppressed*. New York: Continuum Publishing.

Frigault, R., Maloney, G., & Trevino, C. (1986). Training paraprofessionals to facilitate leadership development. *Journal of College Student Personnel, 27*(3), 281–282.

Garland, P. H. (1985). *Serving more than students: A critical need for college student personnel services*. (ASHE-ERIC Higher Education Report No. 7). Washington, DC: Association for the Study of Higher Education.

Garland, P. H., & Grace, T. W. (1993). *New perspectives for student affairs professionals: Evolving realities, responsibilities, and roles*. (ASHE-ERIC Higher Education Report No. 7). Washington, DC: George Washington University School of Education and Human Development.

Giddens, A. (1979). *Central problems in social theory: Action, structure and contradiction in social analysis*. Berkeley: University of California Press.

Gilligan, C. (1982). *In a different voice: Psychological theory and women's development*. Cambridge, MA: Harvard University Press.

Goodsell, A. M., Maher, M., & Tinto, V. (Eds.) (1992). *Collaborative learning: A sourcebook for higher education*. University Park, PA: National Center on Postsecondary Teaching, Learning, and Assessment, Pennsylvania State University.

Guarasci, R. (2001). Recentering learning: An interdisciplinary approach to academic and student affairs. *New Directions for Student Services, 116*, 101–109. San Francisco: Jossey-Bass.

Guba, E. G., & Lincoln, Y. S. (1989). *Fourth generation evaluation*. Thousand Oaks, CA: Sage.

Hamrick, F. A., Evans, N. J., & Schuh, J. H. (2002). *Foundations of student affairs practice: How philosophy, theory, and research strengthen educational outcomes.* San Francisco: Jossey-Bass.

Harding, S. (Ed.). (1987). *Feminism and methodology: Social sciences issues.* Bloomington: Indiana University Press.

Harding, S. (1991). *Whose science? Whose knowledge? Thinking from women's lives.* Ithaca, NY: Cornell University Press.

Hecht, I. D., Higgerson, M. L., Gmelch, W. H., & Tucker, A. (1999). *The department chair as academic leader.* Phoenix, AZ: American Council on Education and Oryx Press.

Hersh, R. H. (1999). Generating ideals and transforming lives: A contemporary case for the residential liberal arts college. *Daedalus, 128*(1), 173–194.

Hirt, J. B., Amelink, C. T., & Schneiter, S. (2004). The nature of student affairs work in the liberal arts college. *NASPA Journal, 42,* 94–110.

Horowitz, H. L. (1987). *Campus life: Undergraduate cultures from the end of the eighteenth century to the present.* Chicago: University of Chicago Press.

Hu, S., & Kuh, G. D. (2002). Being (dis)engaged in educationally purposeful activities: The influence of student and institutional characteristics. *Research in Higher Education, 43,* 555–576.

Hurtado, S., Milem, J., Clayton-Pedersen, A., & Allen, W. (1999). *Enacting diverse learning environments.* (ASHE-ERIC Monograph). Washington, DC: George Washington University.

Javinar, J. M. (2000). Student life and development. *New Directions for Higher Education, 111,* 85–93.

Johnson, D. W., Johnson, R., & Smith, K. A. (1991). *Cooperative learning: Increasing college faculty instructional productivity.* (ASHE-ERIC Higher Education Report No. 4). Washington, DC: George Washington University, School of Education and Human Development.

Kezar, A. (2003a). Achieving student success: Strategies for creating partnerships between academic and student affairs. *NASPA Journal, 41,* 1–22.

Kezar, A. (2003b). Enhancing innovative partnerships: Creating a change model for academic and student affairs collaboration. *Innovative Higher Education, 28,* 137–156.

Kinzie, J., & Kuh, G. D. (2004). Going DEEP: Learning from campuses that share responsibility for student success. *About Campus, 9*(5), 2–8.

Kirp, D. L. (2003). *Shakespeare, Einstein, and the bottom line: The marketing of higher education.* Cambridge, MA: Harvard University Press.

Knock, G. (1988). The philosophical heritage of student affairs. In A. L. Rentz & G. L. Saddlemire (Eds.), *Student affairs functions in higher education* (pp. 4-20). Springfield, IL: Charles C. Thomas.

Komives, S., Lucas, N., & McMahon, T. (1998). *Exploring leadership: For college students who want to make a difference.* San Francisco: Jossey-Bass.

Kuh, G. D. (1996). Guiding principles for creating seamless learning environments for undergraduates. *Journal of College Student Development, 37,* 135–148.

Kuh, G. D. (1999). Setting the bar high to promote student learning. In G. S. Blimling, E. J. Whitt, & Associates (Eds.), *Good practice in student affairs: Principles to foster student learning* (pp. 67–81). San Francisco: Jossey-Bass.

Kuh, G. D. (2001a). Assessing what really matters to student learning: Inside the National Survey of Student Engagement. *Change, 33*(3), 10–17, 66.

Kuh, G. D. (2001b). *The National Survey of Student Engagement: Conceptual framework and overview of psychometric properties.* Bloomington, IN: Indiana University Center for Postsecondary Research.

Kuh, G. D. (2003, March–April). What we're learning about student engagement from NSSE. *Change, 35*(2), 24–32.

Kuh, G., Kinzie, J., Schuh, J., Whitt, E., & Associates. (2005). *Student success in college: Creating conditions that matter.* San Francisco: Jossey-Bass.

Kuh, G., Schuh, J., Whitt, E., & Associates. (1991). *Involving colleges: Successful approaches to fostering student learning and development outside the classroom.* San Francisco: Jossey-Bass.

Kuh, G. D., & Whitt, E. J. (1988). *The invisible tapestry: Culture in American colleges and universities.* (ASHE-ERIC Higher Education Report, No. 1). Washington, DC: Association for the Study of Higher Education.

LeCompte, M. D., & Preissle, J. (1993). *Ethnography and qualitative design in educational research.* San Diego: Academic Press.

Levine, A. (2000, October 27). The future of colleges: 9 inevitable changes. *Chronicle of Higher Education, 47*(9), B10 .

Levine, A., & Cureton, J. S. (1998). *When hope and fear collide.* San Francisco: Jossey-Bass.

Lightfoot, S. L. (1986). On goodness in schools: Themes of empowerment. *Peabody Journal of Education, 63*(3), 9–28.

Lincoln, Y. S., & Guba, E. (1985). *Naturalistic inquiry.* Thousand Oaks, CA: Sage.

Lyons, J. W. (1993). The importance of institutional mission. In M. J. Barr & Associates, *The handbook of student affairs* (pp. 3–15). San Francisco: Jossey-Bass.

Magolda, M. B. B. (1999). Engaging students in active learning. In G. S. Blimling, E. J. Whitt, & Associates, *Good practice in student affairs: Principles to foster student learning* (pp. 21–43). San Francisco: Jossey-Bass.

Magolda, P. M. (2005). Proceed with caution: Uncommon wisdom about academic and student affairs partnerships. *About Campus, 9*(6), 16–21.

Manning, K. (1996). Contemplating the myths of student affairs. *NASPA Journal, 34*(1), 36–46.

Martin, J., & Murphy, S. (2000). *Building a better bridge: Creating effective partnerships between academic affairs and student affairs.* Washington, DC: NASPA.

McKeachie, W. J., Pintrich, P. R., Lin, Y., & Smith, D. (1986). *Teaching and learning in the college classroom: A review of the research.* Ann Arbor, MI: National Center for Research to Improve Postsecondary Teaching and Learning, University of Michigan.

Merriam, S. (2002). *Qualitative research and case study applications in education.* San Francisco: Jossey Bass.

Michalak, S. J., & Robert, J. F. (1981). Research productivity and teaching effectiveness at a small liberal arts college. *Journal of Higher Education, 52*(6), 578–597.

Miller, Margaret A., & Ewell, Peter. (2004). *Measuring Up.* San Jose, CA: National Center for Public Policy and Higher Education.

Morgan, G. (1997). *Images of organization.* Thousand Oaks, CA: Sage.

Mueller, K. H. (1961). *Student personnel work in higher education.* Boston: Houghton Mifflin.

National Association of Student Personnel Administrators. (1989). *Points of view.* Washington, DC.

National Center for Education Statistics. (2004). *The condition of education 2004.* (Issue Brief No. 2004-077). Washington, DC: U.S. Department of Education.

National Center for Education Statistics. (2005). *Postsecondary participation rates by sex and race/ethnicity: 1974–2003.* (Issue Brief No. 2005-028). Washington, DC: U.S. Department of Education.

National Commission on Excellence in Education. (1983). *A nation at risk.* Washington, DC.

National Survey of Student Engagement. (2002). *From promise to progress: How colleges and universities are using student engagement results to improve collegiate quality.* Bloomington: Indiana University Center for Postsecondary Research.

National Survey of Student Engagement. (2003a). *Converting data into action: Expanding the boundaries of institutional improvement.* Bloomington: Indiana University Center for Postsecondary Research.

National Survey of Student Engagement. (2003b). *Final report, Alverno College.* Unpublished paper. Bloomington, IN.

National Survey of Student Engagement. (2003c). *Final report, George Mason University.* Unpublished paper. Bloomington, IN.

National Survey of Student Engagement. (2003d). *Final report, Gonzaga University.* Unpublished paper. Bloomington, IN.

National Survey of Student Engagement. (2003e). *Final report, Longwood University.* Unpublished paper. Bloomington, IN.

National Survey of Student Engagement. (2003f). *Final report, Macalester College.* Unpublished paper. Bloomington, IN.

National Survey of Student Engagement. (2003g). *Final report, University of Maine–Farmington.* Unpublished paper. Bloomington, IN.

National Survey of Student Engagement. (2004a). *Converting data into action: Expanding the boundaries of institutional improvement.* Bloomington: Indiana University Center for Postsecondary Research.

National Survey of Student Engagement. (2004b). *Final report, The Evergreen State University.* Unpublished paper. Bloomington, IN.

National Survey of Student Engagement. (2004c). *Final report, University of Kansas.* Unpublished paper. Bloomington, IN.

Noddings, N. (1984). *Caring: A feminine approach to ethics and moral education.* Berkeley: University of California Press.

Nuss, E. M. (2003). The development of student affairs. In S. Komives & D. Woodard (Eds.), *Student services: A handbook for the profession* (pp. 65–88). San Francisco: Jossey-Bass.

Pace, C. R. (1980). Measuring the quality of student effort. *Current Issues in Higher Education, 2,* 10–16.

Pace, C. R. (1982). *Achievement and the quality of student effort.* Washington, DC: National Commission on Excellence in Education.

Pascarella, E. T. (2001). Identifying excellence in undergraduate education: Are we even close? *Change, 33*(3), 19–23.

Pascarella, E. T., & Terenzini, P. T. (1991). *How college affects students.* San Francisco: Jossey-Bass.

Pascarella, E. T., & Terenzini, P. T. (2005). *How college affects students: A third decade of research.* San Francisco: Jossey-Bass.

Pike, G. R. (1993). The relationship between perceived learning and satisfaction with college: An alternative view. *Research in Higher Education, 34*(1), 23–40.

Pope, R. L., Reynolds, A. L., & Mueller, J. A. (2004). *Multicultural competence in student affairs.* San Francisco: Jossey-Bass.

Price, J. (1999). Merging with academic affairs: A promotion or demotion for student affairs? In J. Schuh & E. Whitt, Partnerships between academic and student affairs. *New Directions for Student Services, 87,* 75–83.

Rentz, A. L., & Saddlemire, G. L. (1988). *Student affairs functions in higher education.* Springfield, IL: Charles C. Thomas Publisher.

Rhatigan, J. J. (2000). The history and philosophy of student affairs. In M. J. Barr, M. J. Desler, & Associates, *The handbook of student affairs administration* (pp. 3–24). San Francisco: Jossey-Bass.

Rhatigan, J. J. (2003). The history and philosophy of student affairs. In S. Komives & D. Woodard (Eds.), *Student services: A handbook for the profession* (pp. 3–24). San Francisco: Jossey-Bass.

Rhatigan, J. J., & Schuh, J. H. (1993). The dean over 75 years: Some key themes. *NASPA Journal, 30,* 83–92.

Richards, L. (2002). *Using N6 in qualitative research.* Melbourne, Australia: QSR International.

Roberts, D. C. (1998). Student learning was always supposed to be the core of our work: What happened? *About Campus, 3*(3), 18–22.

Rudolph, F. (1990). *The American college and university: A history.* Athens, GA: University of Georgia Press.

Saddlemire, G. L. (1988). Student activities. In A. L. Rentz & G. L. Saddlemire (Eds.), *Student affairs functions in higher education.* Springfield, IL: Charles C. Thomas Publishers.

Sandeen, A. (1991). *The chief student affairs officer: Leader, manager, mediator, educator.* San Francisco: Jossey-Bass.

Sandeen, A. (2001). Organizing student affairs divisions. In R. B. Winston, Jr., D. G. Creamer, T. K. Miller, & Associates, *The professional student affairs administrator* (pp. 181–209). New York: Routledge.

Sandeen, A. (2004). Educating the whole student: The growing academic importance of student affairs. *Change, 36*(3), 28–33.

Schlossberg, N. K. (1989). Marginality and mattering: Key issues in building community. *New Directions for Student Services, 48,* 5–15.

Schlossberg, N. K., Lynch, A. Q., & Chickering, A. W. (1989). *Improving higher education environments for adults.* San Francisco: Jossey-Bass.

Schroeder, C. C. (1999a). Forging educational partnerships that advance student learning. In G. S. Blimling, E. J. Whitt, & Associates, *Good practice in student affairs: Principles to foster student learning* (pp. 133–156). San Francisco: Jossey-Bass.

Schroeder, C. C. (1999b). Partnerships: An imperative for enhancing learning and institutional effectiveness. *New Directions for Student Services Sourcebook, 87,* 5–18.

Schroeder, C. C. (2003). How are we doing at engaging students? Charles Schroeder talks to George Kuh. *About Campus, 8*(1), 9–16.

Schroeder, C. C., & Hurst, J. C. (1996). Designing learning environments that integrate curricular and cocurricular experiences. *Journal of College Student Development, 37,* 174–181.

Schuh, J. H. (1999). Guiding principles for evaluating student and academic affairs partnerships. *New Directions for Student Services, 87,* 85–92.

Schuh, J. H., & Upcraft, M. L. (2001). *Assessment practice in student affairs: An application manual.* San Francisco: Jossey-Bass.

Schuh, J. H., & Whitt, E. J. (1999). Creating successful partnerships between academic and student affairs. *New Directions for Student Services, 87.*

Schwartz, R. A. (1997). How deans of women became men. *Review of Higher Education, 20,* 419–436.

Schwartz, R. A. (2002). The rise and demise of deans of men. *Review of Higher Education, 26,* 217–236.

Scott, R. A., & Bischoff, P. M. (2000). Preserving student affairs in times of fiscal constraint: A case history. *NASPA Journal, 38,* 122–133.

Shaffer, R. H. (1961/1986). Student personnel problems requiring a campus-wide approach. In G. L. Saddlemire & A. L. Rentz (Eds.), *Student affairs: A profession's heritage* (pp. 183–191). Alexandria, VA: ACPA.

Simon, H. A. (1957). *Administrative behavior.* New York: Free Press.

Smith, P. (2004). *The quiet crisis: How higher education is failing America.* Boston: Anker.

Society for College and University Planning. (2004, November). *Trends in higher education.* Ann Arbor, MI.

Sorcinelli, M. D. (1991). Research findings on the seven principles. *New Directions for Teaching and Learning, 47,* 13–25.

Strange, C. C., & Banning, J. H. (2001). *Educating by design: Creating campus learning environments that work.* San Francisco: Jossey-Bass.

Study Group on the Conditions of Excellence in American Higher Education. (1984). *Involvement in learning: Realizing the potential of American higher education.* Washington, DC: National Institute of Education.

Tagg, J. (2003). *The learning paradigm college.* Boston: Anker.

Thelin, J. R. (2003). Historical overview of American higher education. In S. R. Komives, D. B. Woodard, Jr., & Associates, *Student services: A handbook for the profession* (4th ed., pp. 3–22). San Francisco: Jossey-Bass.

Thelin, J. R. (2004). *A history of American higher education*. Baltimore: Johns Hopkins University Press.

Tinto, V. (1993). *Leaving college: Rethinking the causes and cures of student attrition* (2nd ed.). Chicago: University of Chicago Press.

Tinto, V. (1996). Reconstructing the first year of college. *Planning for Higher Education, 25*(1), 1–6.

Upcraft, M. L. (1993). Organizational and administrative approaches. In R. B. Winston, Jr., S. Anchors, & Associates, *Student housing and residential life* (pp. 189–202). San Francisco: Jossey-Bass.

Weber, M. (1947). *The theory of social and economic organization*. London: Oxford University Press.

Weick, K. (1976). Educational organizations as loosely-coupled systems. *Administrative Science Quarterly, 21*, 1–21.

Wheatley, M. (1994). *Leadership and the new science: Learning about organization from an orderly universe*. San Francisco: Berrett-Koehler.

Whitt, E. J., & Kuh, G. D. (1991). Qualitative research in higher education: A team approach to multiple site investigation. *Review of Higher Education, 14*, 317–337.

Winston, R. B. & Ender, S. C. (1988). Use of student paraprofessionals in divisions of college student affairs. *Journal of Counseling and Development, 66*(10), 466–473.

Woo, T. O., & Bilynsky, J. (1994). *Involvement in extracurricular activities and adjustment to college*. Washington, DC: ERIC Clearinghouse on Education. (ERIC Document Reproduction Service No. 378474).

Yeater, E. A., Miltenberger, P. A., Laden, M. R., Ellis, S., & O'Donohue, W. (2001). Collaborating with academic affairs: The development of a sexual assault prevention and counseling program within an academic department. *NASPA Journal, 38*, 438–450.

Young, R. B. (1996). Guiding values and philosophy. In S. R. Komives, D. B. Woodard, Jr., & Associates, *Student services: A handbook for the profession* (3rd ed., pp. 83–105). San Francisco: Jossey-Bass.

Zohar, D. (1997). *Rewiring the corporate brain: Using the new science to rethink how we structure and lead organizations*. San Francisco: Berrett-Koehler.

About the Authors

Kathleen Manning has taught as an associate professor at the University of Vermont since 1989 in the Higher Education and Student Affairs (HESA) graduate program. In 2003, she was a Fulbright Fellow at Beijing Normal University in China. She returned to lecture and conduct research in China in 2004 under the Fulbright Senior Specialist Program. She is a recipient of the Kroepsch-Maurice Award for Teaching Excellence, a universitywide teaching award and various awards for professional service. In 2005, the National Association of Student Personnel Administrators selected her as a Pillar of the Profession. Dr. Manning conducts research and writes in the areas of organizational theory, research methodology, and cultural pluralism. Published books include *Research in the College Context: Approaches and Methods* (2003, co-edited with Frances K. Stage); *Rituals, Ceremonies and Cultural Meaning in Higher Education* (2000); *Giving Voice to Critical Campus Issues: Qualitative Research in Student Affairs* (2000); and *Enhancing the Multicultural Campus Environment* (1992, co-authored with Frances K. Stage). Dr. Manning has a Ph.D. in higher education with a minor in anthropology from Indiana University; an M.S. and an Ed.S. in counseling and student personnel services from the State University of New York at Albany; and a B.A. in biology from Marist College.

Jillian Kinzie is associate director of the NSSE Institute for Effective Educational Practice and project manager of the Documenting

Effective Educational Practices (DEEP) initiative. She earned her Ph.D. in Higher Education with a minor in Women's Studies at Indiana University, Bloomington. Prior to this, she held a visiting faculty appointment in the HESA department at Indiana University and worked as assistant dean in an interdisciplinary residential college and as an administrator in student affairs. In 2001, she was awarded a Student Choice Award for Outstanding Faculty at Indiana University. Dr. Kinzie has co-authored a monograph on theories of teaching and learning and has conducted research on women in undergraduate science, retention of underrepresented students, and college choice.

John H. Schuh is Distinguished Professor of Educational Leadership at Iowa State University in Ames, Iowa, where he is also department chair. Previously he has held administrative and faculty assignments at Wichita State University, Indiana University (Bloomington), and Arizona State University. He earned his B.A. in history from the University of Wisconsin-Oshkosh and his Master of Counseling and Ph.D. degrees from Arizona State. He is the author, co-author, or editor of over 200 publications, including 20 books and monographs, 52 book chapters, and 102 articles. Among these are *Foundations of Student Affairs Practice* (2002, with Florence A. Hamrick and Nancy J. Evans), and *Involving Colleges* (1991, with George Kuh, Elizabeth Whitt, and Associates). Currently he is editor-in-chief of the *New Directions for Student Services* sourcebook series and is associate editor of the *Journal of College Student Development*. Schuh has made over 210 presentations and speeches to campus-based, regional, and national meetings and has served as a consultant to 50 colleges, universities, and other organizations. Among his many honors, Schuh has received the Contribution to Knowledge Award and the Presidential Service Award from the American College Personnel Association and was selected as a Pillar of the Profession by the National Association of Student Personnel Administrators in 2001.

Index

A

Academic Affairs, 19
  direct reporting to, benefits of,
    50–51
  merger with Student Affairs, 19–20
academic experience, greater
    accountability for, 21–22
academic institutions
  challenge of technology for, 149
  conditions central to student success,
    23–24, 82, 139–140
  culture and context, 152, 155
  dialogue with students, 138
  fragmentation in, 131–132
  future trends, 148–149
  impact of independent faculty,
    149–150
  public versus private, 61–62
  student support structures, 122
academic mission, 55–56
  and student learning, 122, 129,
    138, 155
administrative approaches to
    Student Affairs practice,

determining factors,
    58–63
bureaucracy, 60, 62–63
communication between divisions,
    62–63
and functional silos, 58, 63–68
institutional mission, 59
institutional size, 58–59
organizational theorists, 59–63
pyramid style, 62f
student services, 58
See also academic/ collaborative
    models
Allen, K., 48, 72
Alverno College, 72
Ambler, D., 13
Amelink, C. T., 15
American Association of Higher
    Education (AAHE), 31
American College Personnel
    Association (ACPA), 23,
    125
American Council on Education
    (ACE), 125
Astin, A. W., 25, 81, 105

B

Ballard, S., 18
Ballou, R. A., 16
Bandura, A., 112
Barr, M. J., 15, 140
Benedict, A., 110
Bischoff, P. M., 16
Blau, P. M., 62, 63
Blimling, G. S., 16
Bologna Declaration, 150–151
Bourassa, D., 125
Bowen, H. R., 89
Boyer, E. L., 11
Breen, D.G., 45
    and campus leadership programs,
        45–46
Brown, R.D., 48, 53, 54, 86, 89, 135

C

campus dissent, 9
Casper, B., 110
Center of Inquiry in the Liberal
    Arts, 31
Chandler, E.M., 9
Cherrey, C., 48, 72
Chickering, A. W., 44
Chorodow, N., 100–101
civil rights unrest, 9
Clothier, Robert C., 38
co-curricular model, 84–88
    defined, 85
    illustrative vignette, 85
    locus of learning , 87–88
    mission, 85
    philosophy of, 86
collaborative models for student affairs
        practice, 122–141
    academic-centered model, 122,
        132–41
        adaptation of academic roles and
            titles, 129–130
        characteristics of, 135–141

educational enrichment, 130,
    133, 141
faculty-student interaction, 139
history, 134–135
illustrative vignette, 132–133
reporting lines, 137
resident assistants, 129
strengths, 138–139
student affairs initiatives and,
    133–134
student affairs support systems,
    134
student success and, 122, 126,
    136–138
weakness of, 139
See also institutional support
    structures
academic-student affairs
        collaboration model,
        122–131
    characteristics of, 126–131
    collaboration between student
        and academic affairs, 124
    expression of partnership, 141
    history, 125
    illustrative vignette, 123–124
    liberal arts colleges and, 135, 136
    mutual respect between student
        and academic affairs,
        124–125
    philosophy of, 125–126
    strengths, 130–131
    student life programs, 127
    student success, 126
    team-oriented learning
        environment, 130
    weaknesses, 130–131
competitive/adversarial model, 79–84
    characteristics of, 79–80, 83–84
    history, 80–81
    illustrative vignette, 80
    philosophy, 82–83
Cowley, W. H., 9
Crane, W. J., 9

D

Dewey, J., 115
Documenting Effective Educational
    Practices (DEEP)
  altered organizational structures,
    129
  data collection, 162–163
  educationally effective
    institutions, 98
  findings, 55, 73–75, 108, 119,
    122, 128–129, 137–138,
    150, 154–155, 156–157,
    160
  funding for, 31
  impact of physical environment on
    learning, 74
  omission of extracurricular model,
    51–52
  project schools, 66, 79
    prevalence of student agency
      model and, 115
    uneven burden of academic-
      student affairs model,
      130–131
  research project outlined, 29–33,
    161–65
  under auspices of NSSE, 161
Doyle, J., 15, 16
Dungy, G. J., 12

E

Education Amendment (1972), Title
    IX, 10
Engstrom, C. M., 19
ethic of care model, 98–103
  acknowledgement of essential
    remedial services, 101
  application to entering freshman
    and transfers, 101
  centrality of student services,
    98–100
  history, 100
  illustrative vignette, 99–100
  strengths, 102
  theoretical underpinnings, 98–102
  weaknesses, 102–103
European Union (EU), 150
Evans, N. J., 13
Evergreen State University, 115
extracurricular model, 39–56
  advantages of, 40–41
  assessment guide, 56
  characteristics of, 46
    and dualistic structure of, 46–47
  dualistic model compared, 47t
  history and characteristics of, 42–43
  illustrative vignettes, 40–41, 42, 43,
    45–46
  leadership development, 45–46
  philosophy of, 41–42
  strengths, 52–53
  theoretical foundations, 43–45
  weaknesses, 48, 53–54

F

Fenske, R., 4
Freire, P., and empowerment models,
    116
Frigault, R., 110
functional silos model, 63–68, 74
  characteristics, 64, 74–75
  illustrative vignette, 64–65, 68
  strengths, 66–67
  weaknesses, 67–68

G

Garland, P.H., 160
GI Bill, 97
Giddens, A., 112
Gilligan, C., 44, 98, 100–101
Gonzaga University, 74
graduate education in student affairs,
    innovative changes, 159–60

Greek organizational structure,
    evolution of, 43
Guarasci, R., 122

H
Harper, W.R., 135
Harvard University, 81
higher education
    transformation of, 145
    and current role of student affairs,
        146–47
higher education organization, dualistic
    model, 47t
Hirt, J. B., 15

I
In a Different Voice, 100
in loco parentis, court challenges, 9
    practical applications of, 9, 58, 102
innovative models for student affairs
    practice, 33–34, 97–119,
        121–141
    See ethic of care model, student
        agency model, student
        driven model
Involvement in Learning, 22

K
Kezar, A., 17
Kruger, K., 125
Kuh, G. D., 11, 25, 90, 155

L
Larson, L., 110
Learning Reconsidered, 23, 158
Levine, A., 148, 149, 150, 152, 154
Lightfoot, L., 116
Littlepage, G., 110

Long, P. N., 18–19
Longwood University, 32
Lumina Foundation for Education, 31
Lyons, J. W., 14

M
Magolda, P.M., 130
*Making Quality Count in Undergraduate
    Education*, 22
Maloney, G., 110
Mattering and Marginality, 107
Miami University, 32
Mueller, K.H., 8, 85

N
National Association of Student
    Personnel Administrators
    (NASPA), 23, 89, 125
National Center for Education
    Statistics (NCES), 82
National Collegiate Athletic
    Association (NCAA)
    Division I, 156
National Survey of Student
    Engagement (NSSE), 24,
    26, 29, 31, 161
Nation at Risk, A, 22
Noddings, N., 98

P
Pace, C. R., 25
Panke, J., 110
Parks, R., 17
Pascarella, E. T., 11, 24, 106
Perspective on Student Affairs, A, 53
Pieces of Eight, 146
Points of View, 89
*Powerful Partnership: A Shared
    Responsibility*, 11, 23, 121,
    151, 158

Principles of Good Practice for Student Affairs, 11, 15, 27, 151
principles of learning, 16–17

R

Ramapo College, 16
Reason, R. D., 13
Rehabilitation Act of 1973, 10
Reliance on Psychosexual Student Development Models, 44
"Residential Nexus, The," 23
Rhatigan, J. J., 10, 41
Roberts, D.C., 125
Rudolph, F., 105

S

Sandeen, A., 9, 12, 15, 50–51, 140
Scaffer, R.H., 11
Schlossberg, N.K., 107
Schneiter, S., 15
Schroeder, C.C., 17, 82
Schub, J. H., 11
Schwartz, R. A., 9–10
Scott, R. A., 16
seamless learning model, 40, 55, 88–93
    elements of, 79, 90–93
    history, 89
    illustrative vignette, 78–79, 88–90
    philosophy, 90
    preference of research team, 92
    See also DEEP
Serving More Than Students, 160
"Seven Principles for Good Practices in Undergraduate Education, The," 22
Smith, P., 22
Student Affairs Functions in Higher Education, 61
Student Affairs practice
    approaches to, 13–14, 98
    collaboration, barriers to, 17–18
    core values, 6, 56

defined, 38–39
development of, 4–5, 58–59
educationally effective practice, 33–34
functions of, 4–5, 6–7, 11–12, 61, 81
goals, 55
growing importance of, 138
historical view, 3–5
holistic approach, 48
increasing complexity, 8–14, 30
institutional mission and, 12, 14–15, 75
learning-centered approaches, 75
liberal arts colleges, interaction with, 15
organization of, 11–12, 49
    entity in Academic Affairs, 49f
oversight, 12–13
pluralism and tolerance, promotion of, 153
practice, evolution of, 7–8, 30, 39, 46–47
professional endeavor, 3–4, 140
reform in, 29, 148
reporting models, 49–51
responsibilities, 28–29, 57–58
strategies, 17–18
student/academic partnerships, 121–22
traditional approaches, saliency of, 75
transformation from traditional to innovative models, 156–60
    and catalysts for change, 156
women in, 61
    See also collaborative models; innovative models; traditional models
student agency model, 111–118
    characteristics of, 114, 118
    collaboration among students, faculty, and administrators, 114
    defined, 111, 112, 113
    empowerment of students, 112–113

graduation rates and, 119
history, 112
illustrative vignette, 111–12
and institutional mission, 114
learning paradigms, 140
mentoring, 117
strengths, 116–17
student initiative, 118
weaknesses, 117–118
student-centered learning, 27
student driven model, 103–111
  adaptations to, 110
  basic assumptions of, 103
  centrality of student involvement,
    104–105, 107–108
  history, 105
  illustrative vignette, 103–104
  marginality and integration,
    107–108
  paraprofessional service, 105
    benefits and challenges of,
      109–111
student employment, on campus versus
    off campus, 107
  paid and unpaid, 110
  training and supervision, 110
  valuing contribution, 107–108
  student engagement defined, 106
  strengths, 108–109, 110
  theoretical underpinning, 105–108
    and Astin, 105–106
  weaknesses, 109–111
student engagement, 24–26
Student Learning Imperative, The, 11, 17,
    23, 27, 53, 63, 74, 89, 90,
    125, 126, 151, 152, 158
Student Personnel Point of View, The
    (1937), 5, 6, 39, 41, 60, 125,
    126, 135, 158
Student Personnel Point of View, The
    (1949), 5, 6, 60–61, 125–26,
    135
  central principles of, 7
*Student Services: A Handbook for the
    Profession*, 61

student services model, 68–73, 74
  characteristics of, 68–70
  and financial services, 68–69
  illustrative vignette, 70
  strengths, 70–71
  weaknesses, 71–73, 75
  See also administrative-centered
    approaches to student affairs
    practice
student success, formula for retention,
    25–28
  conditions for, 33t
  defined, 22–23, 27
  expectations for performance, 25
  factors in, 23
  institutional conditions outlined,
    23–24, 25
*Student Success in College: Creating
    Conditions That Matter*, 29,
    31
student union facilities, 43
Study Group on the Conditions of
    Excellence in American
    Higher Education (1984),
    89

T

Tagg, J., 140
technology, impact on student learning,
    157–58
Terenzini, P.T., 11, 25
Thelin, J. R., 10
Tinto, J., 19, 52, 107
traditional models for student affairs,
    33–34, 37–93
  See co-curricular model,
    competitive/adversarial
    model, extracurricular
    model, functional silos
    model, seamless learning model,
    student services model
Trenton State College (College of New
    Jersey), 72
Trevino, C., 110

U

University of Kansas, 66, 115,
University of Maine at Farmington
      Student Work Initiative,
      31–32, 61–62, 73–74
University of Pennsylvania, 43
University of Texas at El Paso, 32

V

Vice President of Student Affairs,
      management responsibilities
      of, 57–58
Vietnam War, 9

W

Wabash College, 31
Weber, M., 59
Weick, K., 127
and coupling, 127–28
Wheatley, M., 48
Whitt, E. J., 11, 16, 155

Y

Young, R. B., 82

Z

Zohar, D., 48

CPSIA information can be obtained at www.ICGtesting.com
Printed in the USA
BVOW021555210911

271769BV00003B/261/P